Martin Lohse

Bach Counterpoint

Two-part invention I

The Royal Danish Academy of Music

2021

Bach Counterpoint – Two-part invention I

Published by:
The Royal Danish Academy of Music • 2021
Rosenørns Allé 22
1970 Frederiksberg C

Second edition, first print (first edition published 2019)
ISBN: 978-87-87131-14-8
Copyright: Martin Lohse

Editor: Anne Heide
Translation: Tuan Hao Tan
Printed by: Kindle Direct Publishing

Preface

The music theory environment at The Royal Danish Academy of Music is a special one. Its history can be traced back to the start of the 20th Century. The groundbreaking writings of Knud Jeppesen (1892-1974), *The Style of Palestrina and the Dissonance* (1922) and *Counterpoint* (1930) became the foundation of a steadily growing tradition. Within this tradition, thorough and detailed analyses of original music are used as the starting point for compositional studies based on individual compositional styles from the Renaissance to contemporary music. This creative environment was established by great exponents of music theory, such as Finn Høffding (1899-1997), Povl Hamburger (1901-1972), and Svend Westergaard (1922-1988), who all had close ties with The Royal Danish Academy of Music. Even today, this environment is still an essential part of the The Royal Danish Academy of Music, and their work has been carried on by, amongst others, Yngve Jan Trede (1933-2010), Niels La Cour (1944-), Lars Bisgaard (1947-), and not to mention, my own teacher, Niels Rosing-Schow (1954-). *Counterpoint - Two-part invention in the style of Bach* carries on this long music theoretical tradition. Without this academic environment, and the passing down of knowledge from teacher to student through the generations, this book in two volumes would not have been written.

I would like to express my thanks to my colleauge, Thorkil Mølle, for his commendable work in reading through the text, as well as playing through all examples. His insights and comments have been invaluable in this process.

I would also like to specially thank Tuan Hao Tan, who has translated this book to English. An essential part of translating this book has been transferring music theoretical concepts and symbols from a Danish to English context. Tuan Hao's deep understanding of music theory has been a great help here, for example, in translating Functional Analysis, and the related symbols, to English.

I would also like to express my warmest gratitude to Anne Heide for her work in editing this book, and not to mention my wife, Pia Thomsen. Her keen eye and feedback, always clearly articulated, have lifted this book from being just a textbook to an aid in gaining insight into '*the compositional workshop*', where notes become music, and music, hopefully, becomes art.

Finally, I would like to express my deepest gratitude to The Royal Danish Academy of Music, which has supported this process both financially and with its resources. Without this support, it would not have been possible to write or publish this book.

In this second edition, minor errors and omissions have been corrected, and the section on mediant chords (p. 93-97) has been rewritten.

Martin Lohse, Frederiksberg 8th of October 2021

Table of Contents

Introduction

This book is divided into two volumes. In the first volume, the art of writing an invention in the style of Bach is introduced, and through that, a deeper insight and understanding of the harmonic, motivic, and contrapuntal richness of Bach's music can be obtained.

Contrapuntal development is one of the most difficult disciplines in music theory, but also one of the most rewarding. Studying contrapuntal development can heighten the compositional skill and understanding of the compositional process for both the creative as well as the performing artist.

In the teaching of composition, three-part *Bach fugues* are traditionally used to introduce the topic of contrapuntal composition. Bach fugues are regarded, rightly so, as the pinnacle of the Baroque polyphonic style, and they are therefore a stylistic genre, which both performing and creative artists strive to master. In terms of didactics and paedagogy, Bach fugues are, however, a difficult and complicated style to begin with; the compositional possibilities are many, and it can be overwhelming having to work with a minimum of three voices.

The aim of this book is to explain Bach's compositional methods in an accessible manner, using methods and tools specially developed for this purpose.

The two-part Bach inventions are a natural starting point, and have certain clear advantages when used to illustrate Baroque contrapuntal composition; it is in two parts, its form is clear, and it contains the same compositional techniques as the fugue, such as countermelody/counterpoint, sequences and motivic development.

Volume I will mainly focus on the first section of the form, up to the entry of the theme in the dominant or tonic parallel tonality. While relatively short, this will prove sufficient in introducing Bach's music. The exercises in this volume include writing counterpoint to a given melody, composing a longer sequence that concludes in a cadence in the new tonality, and will also cover topics such as melodic development, rhythm, and the treatment of dissonance in the style of Bach.

In *Volume II*, instruction in compositional development continues with the analysis and composition of complete inventions, including the first section of the form, which is covered in this volume.

What do we know about Bach's inventions?

The literature regarding Bach's inventions is relatively thin, and is mainly comprised of analyses of differing degrees of detail. However, there are rather few descriptions of *how* inventions are written. This book fills this niche, and develops a method of understanding and composing inventions, based on a throrough analysis and exploration of Bach's inventions.

To illustrate the progression and stringency of this method, this book has been structured as an insight into the 'compositional workshop'. Through analyses and music examples, the process of creation is illustrated, and throughout the book, *how* and *why* musical decisions are made are explained.

As a result of the richness in the motivic and harmonic development of Bach's own inventions, no two inventions are similar. This means that both the creative as well as performing artist have to be conscious of the fact that the method in this book is both didactic and paedagogical, but very strict in terms of artistically understanding Bach's music. In the creation of live music, artistic ideas and natural variations arise, and these are beyond the scope of this book.

Volume I is divided into three sections, and is supplimented with a number of appendices:

1. **Voice-leading in the style of Bach**, including the treatment of dissonance, rhythm, and melody

2. **Minor tonality inventions**, first section

3. **Major tonality inventions**, first section

   Appendices A-E

Exercises

This book can be used as self-study material, but is best suited to be used in the classroom, where the student's work with inventions can be corrected and evaluated.

Appendix E comprises themes of invention that are suited to the exercises in *Volume I* and *II*.

In the section on minor tonality inventions, 3-5 minor themes should be worked on, and the same themes should be used in all chapters. In this manner, 3-5 inventions will be written, covering the development of counterpoint, sequence, variation of the sequence, cadential preparation, and finally, cadence.

With the major tonality inventions, one theme should be worked on at a time, so that a longer and more consistent compositional process can be experienced.

Advice from the author: it is always best to compose these inventions with a piano. The rewards are significant, and the understanding gained of Bach's contrapuntal style is richer than a purely theoretical perspective of Bach's music.

The theoretical and methodological starting point of this book

The creation of this book arose out of the fact that the exploration and analysis of Bach's contrapuntal works will, in itself, lead to answers to a range of theoretical and methodological questions. Questions on form, proportion, harmonic progression, the treatment of dissonance, voice-leading, and so on are therefore not theoretically isolated, but explored through deep empirical analyses of Bach's two-part inventions. Methodologically, the approach is thus far more empirical than theoretically grounded.. This means that the arguments put forth in this book are based on analyses of the great richness and diversity in the compositional techniques used by Bach. This exemplary method of analysis involves comparing and elevating the techniques to represent general trends in Bach's contrapuntal music. In other words, the reader is taken by the hand and, with the power of example, on an inductive journey into Bach's music.

To illustrate this method, and to give insight into Bach's compositional process with counterpoint, this book is supplemented with numerous examples, which have been developed to illustrate the progression of this method and, as previously mentioned, to show *how* compositional challenges are overcome in practice. In other words, these music examples illustrate in detail how contrapuntal problems are solved.

Voice-leading

The essence of composing a beautiful movement in the style of Bach is the mastery of voice-leading – the mastery of the interplay, note for note, between the individual voices in the movement.

In the following section, voice-leading in a two-part Baroque movement will be presented, with special focus on Bach's inventions. This section is divided into different topics, some of which are relevant for general voice-leading, and some of which are independent aspects of voice-leading:

- **General voice-leading** (page 10): The characteristics and range of the harpsichord, and intervals between voices

- **The treatment of dissonance** (page 14): Suspensions and non-chord tones

- **Rhythm** (page 20): Fast and slow rhythms, and complementary rhythms

- **Melodic development** (page 22): Stepwise motion, arpeggiation/broken chord movement, and hidden polyphony

General voice-leading

The piano music of Bach was originally written for harpsichord, but is now commonly performed on the piano. The harpsichord is sounded by mechanically plucking strings when keys are depressed. The harpsichord therefore has a completely different and crisp tone colour as compared to the modern piano.

Important: The harpsichord cannot sound a single tone at different dynamic levels; all tones are sounded with the same dynamic, regardless of how hard the keys are depressed. It is possible to switch between different registers, and thus between *f* - *forte* and *p* - *piano* (for instance), but this requires an amount of time and is not used in the middle of a Baroque movement, unless the movement clearly changes character.

Range

The typical range of the Baroque harpsichord is:

A few instances in the music of Bach go as low as A1, but as a rule, music written in this style should be kept within the range C2 → C6.

Ex. 1, ML: Range

Intervals

In two-part Bach inventions, the underlying harmony, comprising triads and chords with 4 notes, becomes apparent through the liveliness of the music. Chord-tones that are not sounded on the beat are quickly sounded in one of the voices, thus completing the chord.

Even in the slower movements, the underlying harmony can easily be found, as there is clear focus on the "most important" tones in the chord; root, third, and perhaps the dissonance. The following trends are quite natural in two-part music:

The interval of a unison, fifth and octave is often avoided on a strong beat in the bar (first and third in 4/4 and first in 3/8)

Thus, on the strong beat, it follows that the following tones are sounded:

- Root in the bass and third in the soprano or the vice-versa

- Root or third in the bass and seventh in the soprano or vice-versa

- Third in the bass and ninth in the soprano or vice-versa

Overview

	Common		Occasional	Infrequent
Soprano	3rd and 7th	root, 7th and 9th	root and 3rd	3rd
Bass	root	3rd	7th	9th

Bare intervals on the strong beats in the bar (unison, fifth and octave), can occasionally be seen in Bach's works, but there will almost always be a reason for their use to be found in the voice-leading of individual parts.

On the relatively strong beats (second and fourth in 4/4 and second and third in 3/8), intervals of a unison, fifth, and octave are more common, but a better solution can often be found. On weak ♪ and ♫, bare intervals are not a problem.

Parallel intervals

By avoiding, as far as possible, the intervals of a unison, fifth, or octave between the two voices, the chances of writing illegal parallel intervals are reduced.

Parallel octaves and fifths

Parallel unisons, fifths, and octaves should be completely avoided.

Ex. 2, ML: Parallel octaves and fifths

Parallel intervals on strong beats

Ex. 3, ML: Parallel intervals on accented beats

These arise when the interval of an octave or fifth is separated by a ♪ or a ♩.

Parallel fifths on strong beats can be found in the music of Bach, but should be avoided.

Hidden parallels

Ex. 4, ML: Hidden parallels

These arise when the soprano voice leaps <u>and</u> both voices approach an octave or fifth through similar motion.

Hidden parallels are occasionally seen in the music of Bach, but how clearly disccernible they are often depend on the context. Listen!

Voice-leading

Fifth of the chord in the bass

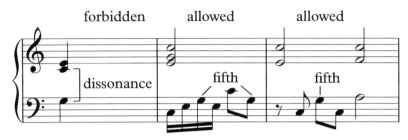

Ex. 5, ML: Fifth of the chord in the bass

In two-part music, the fifth of the chord in the bass should be avoided on strong beats in the bar. It can only be sounded in the bass if it is part of an arpeggio, or part of a theme that moves from the fifth to the root. This is because the interval of a fourth is heard as a dissonance, when it is sounded between the bass and another voice.

In a polyphonic movement with three or more voices, the fifth in the bass is sometimes used as a cadential chord, where **T** with the fifth in the bass is heard as a **D 6/4**. (see also *Appendix A, functional analysis, chords and chord symbols*, ex. 107, page 89)

The treatment of dissonance

Disonnances in the music of Bach can generally be divided into two categories:

1. Suspensions, where one chord tone from the previous chord is tied over as a seventh or ninth

2. Non-chord tones, which arise from the voice-leading of individual voices

Suspension

Ex. 6, ML: Suspension

Suspensions originate from the Renaissance, where they were an important part of the expression and construction of religious modal music. A tone is prepared (**p**), and the dissonance (**d**) occurs between the original tone and the "counter-tone" (**ct**) on a strong beat, followed by the resolution (**r**), which is achieved by the prepared tone moving a step down. The pattern can continue, with the resolved tone being prepared for a new dissonance, and so on. Thus, a chain of dissonances can be formed. (see ex. 6)

In tonal music from the Baroque and after, chain of dissonances are combined with the descending fifth sequence:

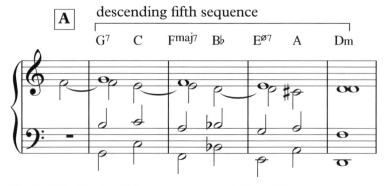

Ex. 7, ML: Chain of dissonances as a falling fifth sequence

(**A**) The most common form: suspensions as sevenths in one of the top voices, here in the alto.
(**B**) Less common: suspensions in the bass.

In the Baroque, suspensions are often used in sequences, but they can also be used in other ways. However, a common characteristic is that notes of ornamentation are often added between the dissonance and its resolution.

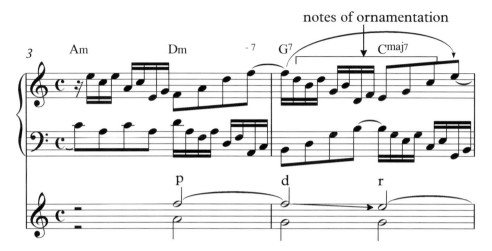

Ex. 8, Bach: Invention no. 13 in A minor, bar 3-4, suspension

In this example, a suspension is prepared on the last ♪ in the first bar, while the resolution of the dissonant tone (f) is heard on the last ♪ of the second bar, with many notes of ornamentation between the dissonance and the resolution.

Upon closer examination, all the chords have the seventh sounded on the last ♪ of the suspension.

Non-chord tones

As seen in the previous example, a distinction can be made between the longer, tied, dissonance that is sounded against a chord and shorter non-chord tones, which arise through the voice-leading of individual parts. These 'local' dissonances are a colouration of the chords, they sound against, as opposed to the suspension, that changes the quality of the chord through the addition of a seventh, ninth, etc.

Important: The easiest treatment of dissonance is to use stepwise motion, possibly with the addition of the occasional third (see also *Stepwise motion* under *Melodic development* on page 22). In this way, the dissonance is prepared, either from above or below, and is resolved through step, as it should be.

Passing tone

The passing tone is the most common non-chord tone and occurs in stepwise motion on weak ♪ or ♪ beats.

Ex. 9, ML: Passing tone

Accented passing tone

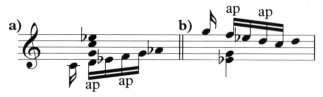

Like the ordinary passing tone, the accented passing tone occurs in stepwise motion, but on accented ♪ or ♪ beats. Thus, the effect is much more pronounced.

Ex. 10, ML: Accented passing tone

Neighbour tone

Neighbour tones are often sounded on ♪ beats, both weak and relatively strong, but not on strong beats.

Ex. 11, ML: Neighbour tone

Suspension and retardation

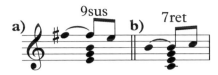

Ex. 12, ML: Suspension and retardation

A suspension can also occur outside the context of a chain of dissonances. The dissonance is, as mentioned above, prepared, sounded against the chord, and resolved through a downward step. An upward resolution can also be found – this is known as a retardation. In this case **b)**, the dissonance functions as a temporary leading tone, which is "retarded" and resolves to the root.

Note of ornamentation

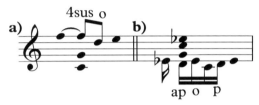

Ex. 13, ML: Ornamentation

Notes of ornamentation are non-chord tones sounded between a dissonance and its resolution. This is also used as a general name for all tones, that are sounded between a dissonance and its resolution, as seen in **b)** or in Bach's A minor invention, ex. 8 page 15, where many notes of ornamentation were seen between the suspension and its resolution.

Anticipation

Ex. 14, ML: Anticipation

The note of anticipation is a non-chord tone, which anticipates the following harmony through the repetition of tones. This dissonance is often used with cadences.

Escape tone and appoggiature

An escape tone is a dissonance that is resolved by leap instead of step **a)**. A dissonance that is not prepared **b)** is referred to as an appoggiatura.

Ex. 15, ML: Escape tone, appoggiatura

Escape tones that are resolved by leap (ex. **a**) are relatively common, while appoggiaturas are rather seldom, and they often arise through polyphonic voice-leading (see also *Melodic development* on page 25).

Pedal tone

pedal tone: **ped**

Ex. 16, Bach: Invention no. 4 in D minor, bar 29-34, pedal tone

The pedal tone is an unchanging tone in the bass sounded against changing harmonies. Thus, the pedal tone will at certain points create a dissonance against the harmony. The pedal tone is often the fifth or root of the tonality, but other tones in the relevant tonality can also be used. This technique is seldom used in the first section of an invention, but is effective in the last section of an invention. In functional analysis, the scale degree of the pedal tone is noted, and the pedal tone itself is not included in the analysis.

Inverted pedal tone

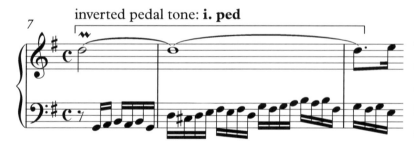

inverted pedal tone: **i. ped**

The inverted pedal tone is similar to the pedal tone, but is sounded in one of the other voices instead of the bass. It should thus be treated in the same manner as a pedal tone.

Ex. 17, Bach: Invention no. 7 in E minor, bar 7-9, inverted pedal tone

Examples

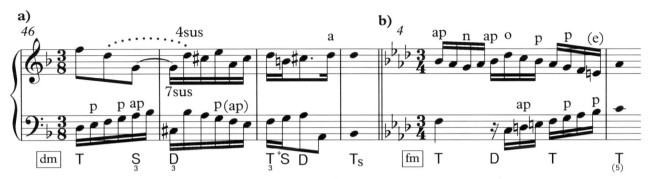

Ex. 18, Bach: Invention no. 4 in D minor, bar 46-47 and invention no. 9 in F minor, bar 4

In **a)**, bar 47, two suspensions in the top voice can be seen:

1. A 7-6 suspension is prepared as normal from a tied note, and is apparently not resolved. The resolution is actually present when the seventh is overtaken and resolved on the third beat in the bass. This is a manoeuvre sometimes seen in the music of Bach, but should be used with care.

2. The 4-3 suspension is prepared from the *d* in the previous bar (marked with a dotted line).

In **b)**, one of the relatively rare dissonant notes of ornamentation is used in the top voice, and an escape tone is sounded on the last ♪ in the bar. However, it is also possible to interpret the last ♪ as a chord change to an incomplete dominant, followed by a rather uncommon leap from the leading tone to the third of the tonic.

Rhythm

A ♪ is the shortest note values used in the inventions of Bach. Certain inventions use ♬, such as the E major Invention no. 6, appendix C, page 115, but in these cases, a special rhythmic idea is often present, and the tempo is also slower. Generally, the shortest note value should be a ♪.

Fast rhythms

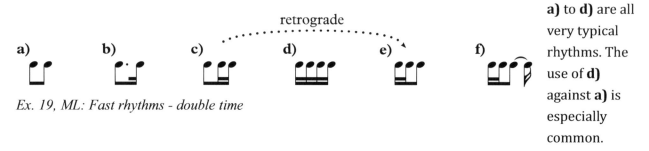

a) to **d)** are all very typical rhythms. The use of **d)** against **a)** is especially common.

Ex. 19, ML: Fast rhythms - double time

e) is the retrograde of **c)**, and should be sparingly used. It halts the rhythmic flow and emphasises the weak ♪ beat. In practice, it is often used in the form of **f)** where the ♪ is tied over as a suspension, thus gaining energy and character from the halted rhythmic energy.

The same rhythms are used in 3/8 as in 4/4.

Ex. 20, ML: Fast rhythms – triple time

All of the above rhythms are common in triple time, with the exception of **x)** that should be treated like **e)** in ex. 19. In **x')**, the first ♪ is extended with with a dot, as in **f)** in the previous example.

Repetition of tones

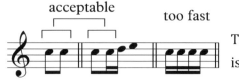

The repetition of tones works well using ♪, but is too fast when ♬ is used.

Ex. 21, ML: Repetition of tones

Slow rhythms

Ex. 22, ML: Slow rhythms

♩ motion **a)** is slightly too heavy for the style of Bach, and is seldom used. Thus, individual ♩ should be used with care. However, the use of ♩ is acceptable when tied to a shorter note value **b)**. The same applies to ♩ **c)**.

Ties

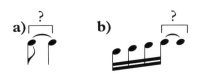

Ex. 23, ML: Ties

Ties are often used in conjunction with suspensions, but can also be used without dissonances.

a) A note may not be tied to a longer note-value.

b) A ♪ can never be tied over.

Complementary rhythms

Ex. 24, Bach: Invention no. 9 in F minor, bar 1-2, complementary rhythms

This is a central concept and one of the stylistic characteristics of Baroque music. It adds rhythmic flow to the music by ensuring that at least one voice maintains a fast rhythm. When the top voice moves in ♪ or longer, the lower voice uses ♪ (or vice-versa). As such, a quick ♪ motion is constantly heard.

Both voices in an invention can move simultaeneously in ♪, but not for too long, as the music becomes too heavy.

The term *complementary rhythms* is occasionally used to describe more general principles, such as the varying use of rhythm between theme and counterpoint, the rhythmic difference between the sections in a movement, or significant rhythmic differences between movements in a work.

Melodic development

One of the most important melodic principles in the music of Bach is balance. After an upward motion, a downward motion is required, and vice-versa. This is especially important in the case of leaps. A leap should be followed by motion in the opposite direction, preferably sounding the tones encompassed by the leap. This is even more so in the case of upward leaps, which should be followed by downward motion.

These melodic principles become even more clear when fast rhythms are used. Thus, in Bach's inventions, they are most apparent in ♪ motion.

There are 3 basic forms of melodic development:

1. Stepwise motion, possibly with few leaps of a third

2. Arpeggiation/broken chord movement

3. Hidden polyphony

Stepwise motion

Stepwise motion is most common, with ♪ and ♪ motion, with small turns and the occasional addition of a third.

The treatment of dissonance in relatively fast stepwise motion is generally rather simple, as all dissonances are 'local' and thus prepared and resolved stepwise down- or upward (see also *Non-chord tones*, page 16-19). Even with the addition of thirds, most dissonances will be treated correctly, possibly with the addition of a single note of ornamentation between the preparation and dissonance, or the dissonance and resolution.

When composing, play, listen, and pay attention to the underlying harmony in the form of chords on the piano, and if the dissonant tones are not too harsh, the treatment of dissonance should be acceptable.

Ex. 25, Bach: Invention no. 9 in F minor, bar 7-8, and Sinfonia no. 1 in C major, bar 1, stepwise motion

Ex. 26, ML: Stepwise motion and turns in the space of a crotchet

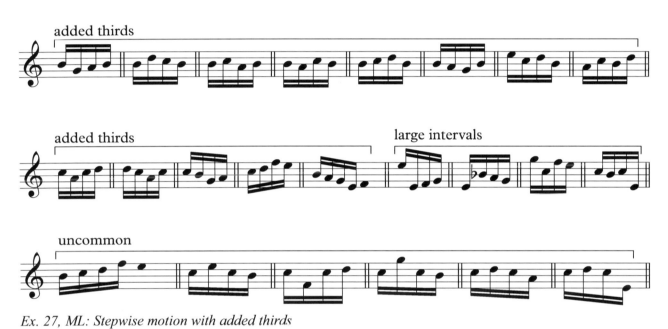

Ex. 27, ML: Stepwise motion with added thirds

Important: If ♪ are used between two ♩, and the next note cannot be reached with stepwise motion, add a leap of a third or use the rhythm ♩♫, for example:

Ex. 28, ML: Filling out crotchet with semiquaver

Zigzag motion is often used in a combination of leap and stepwise motion, and is in itself a good example of balance in melodic development, where a leap is followed by motion in the opposite direction.

Ex. 29, ML: Zigzag motion with stepwise motion

Arpeggiation/broken chord movement

Arpeggiation is commonly used in the music of Bach, both in ♪ and ♪ motion, and the underlying harmony is made very clear through its use.

Pay attention to the *e* in F#m7, which is prepared from the beginning of the bar, and thus functions as a long suspension that is resolved downwards in the next bar.

Ex. 30, Bach: Invention no. 12 in A major, bar 5, arpeggio in semiquaver and quaver

Combining stepwise motion and arpeggiation

This works very well, but should be used with care, as the melody can easily lose the characteristics of a Bach invention.

Ex. 31, Bach: Invention no. 7 in E minor, bar 16, stepwise motion with arpeggiation

Important: When starting out writing music in the style of Bach, *either* stepwise motion *or* arpeggiation should be used for each ♩ in the individual voices. This makes developing the melody easier to approach and develops the ear's sense in the style of Bach.

Hidden polyphony

Hidden polyphony is found in monophonic melodies, which have an underlying polyphonic structure. This is a characteristic form of melodic development, which is often heard in Baroque music, especially in solo works, such as the Bach suites for strings etc.

The principle is seen in many forms, and is not restricted to the Baroque music. It is found in all periods including contemporary music, and is characteristic in the creation of melodic movement, regardless of period and musical style.

Hidden polyphony is especially suited to emphasise the underlying harmony, as an extra voice is added to make harmonic progressions, tied dissonances, and other features clearer.

Ex. 32, Bach: Invention no. 4 in D minor, bar 1-2, hidden polyphony

In this invention theme by Bach, a movement from the root *d* (bar 1) to the leading tone *c#* (bar 2) is clearly heard. At the same time, hidden tie from the highest tone *Bb* to *a*, thus giving the two-part motion as seen in the following bars.

Cadence

Hidden polyphony is commonly used at cadences, where a two-part invention becomes a three-part in its inner stucture, and thus harmonically fuller.

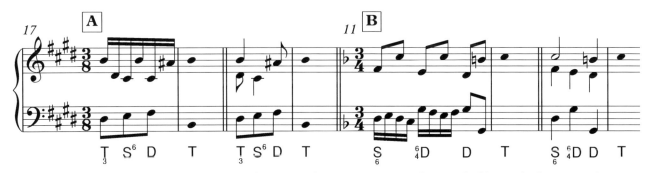

Ex. 33, Bach: Invention no. 6 in E major, bar 17 and no. 8 in F major, bar 11, hidden polyphony - cadences

Sequence

Hidden polyphony is often used at sequences to make harmonies and any possible tied dissonances clearer.

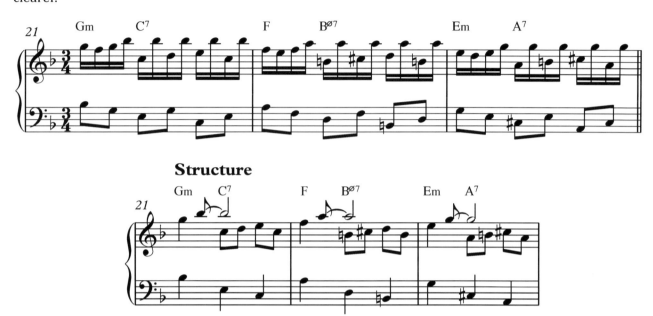

Ex. 34, Bach: Invention no. 8 in F major, bar 21-23, hidden polyphony – sequence

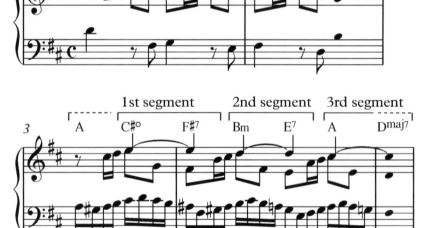

The first section of this theme by Bach is in itself a short sequence with hidden polyphony in the top voice.

The theme is answered a fourth under in the lower voice (see ex. 35). The soprano has long tied notes, thus making the two-part structure apparent.

Ex. 35, Bach: Sinfonia no. 3 in D-dur, bar 1-3, hidden polyphony – sequence

Minor tonality, first section

Bach's own foreword to his two- and three-part inventions:

"Forthright instruction, wherewith lovers of the clavier, especially those desirous of learning, are shown in a clear way not only 1) to learn to play two voices clearly, but also after further progress 2) to deal correctly and well with three obbligato parts, moreover at the same time to obtain not only good ideas, but also to carry them out well, but most of all to achieve a cantabile style of playing, and thereby to acquire a strong foretaste of composition ."[1]

The invention is not a form in itself; like the fugue, it is a compositional technique defined by Bach's two-part, and to a certain extent, three-part, inventions. Originally, *Invention* was used in the sense of 'to invent', without connotation of a certain form or compositional technique. However, in the case of Bach, it has become a compositional technique, which, while similar to the fuge, often uses answers at the octave, and is constrained to a smaller scale.

As mentioned in the foreword, this book will only touch upon two-part invention. The focus is on instrumental and relatively fast themes, which last 1-1½ bars in 4/4 and 2-3 bars in 3/8. The themes in this section will naturally only be in minor.

Through analysing the relevant parts of Bach's inventions, the basic building blocks of contrapuntal development in Bach's style - the elements of the compositional workshop - are made clear.

---

1   Goodfriend, James (2015). *in Glenn Gould Remastered: The Complete Columbia Album Collection.* New York: Sony Classical. p. 136.

Analysis: Bach: Invention no. 4 in D minor, section I

Bach's Invention no. 4 in D minor is in 3/8 and in a fast tempo. A short theme lasting two bars is presented in the soprano in bar 1.

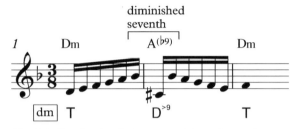

Ex. 36, Bach: Analysis, exposition: Invention no. 4 in D minor, bar 1-3, theme

The theme changes harmony in every bar, and mainly comprises stepwise motion in ♪, that creates a beautiful arc from the root in the tonic tonality (bar 1) to the third (bar 3)

One of the characteristics of the theme is the leap from the lowered sixth degree down to the leading tone and back up again. Using the defining characteristic of a minor tonality, the diminished seventh between the lowered sixth degree and the leading tone, this leap thus frames the entire theme.

In bar 3, the theme is answered an octave below in the bass, while the soprano continues with a counterpoint in ♪ motion, which complements the ♪ motion in the theme. This counterpoint is, as opposed to the stepwise motion in the theme, based on the arpeggiation of **T** in bar 3 and the incomplete **D** in bar 4, and it leads from the third, *f*, in bar 3 to the root, *d*, in bar 5.

Ex. 37, Bach: Analysis, exposition: Invention no. 4 in D minor, bar 3-5, counterpoint

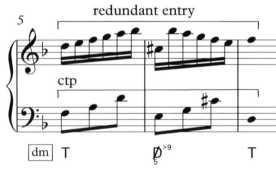

Ex. 38, Bach: Analysis, exposition: Invention no. 4 in D minor, bar 5-7, redundant entry

The soprano has a redundant entry in bar 5. This entry is sounded an octave above the first entry in the soprano, thus making it fresh, and prepares the voices for a long and falling descending fifth sequence in the following bars.

The counterpoint in the bass is almost the same as in bars 3-4, with the exception of it leading to the low *d* in bar 7, thus giving the following sequence a deep bass.

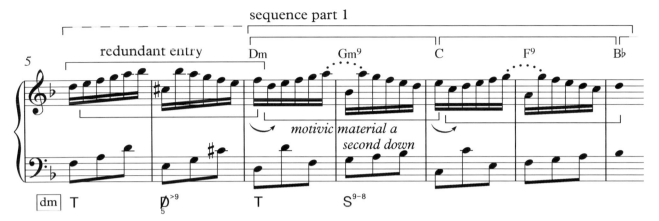

Ex. 39, Bach: Analysis, exposition: Invention no. 4 in D minor, bar 5-11, descending fifth sequence part 1

In bar 7, a two-section descending fifth sequence begins. This sequence is based on the theme (bars 5-7), which is shifted down a second in every other bar, as well as the ♪ in the counterpoint, which are partly changed to stepwise motion. The redundant entry of bars 5-7 is thus heard motivically as a part of the sequence, although the harmonic sequance only begins in bar 7.

Pay attention to how the motivic material from the theme changes harmonically from **T → D** in bars 5-6 to **T → S** in bars 7-8. This change arises from the simple shifting of the motivic material a second down, which is harmonically possible as a result of the theme mainly being in stepwise motion. Thus, the unaccented passing tones are changed into accented passing tones in bar 7 (see also the treatment of dissonance ex. 9-10 page 16 and stepwise motion page 22). As another interesting example of the treatment of dissonance in Baroque music, examine how the ninth in G minor on the second ♪ in bar 8 is prepared in the last ♪ of bar 7. This is also seen in bars 9-10 with the F⁹ harmony.

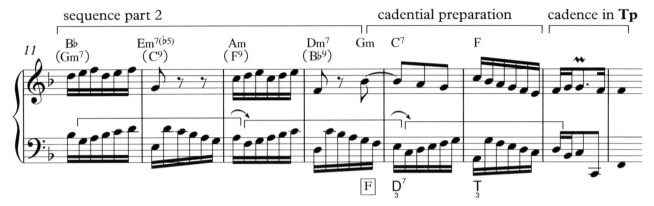

Ex. 40, Bach: Analysis, exposition: Invention no. 4 in D minor, bar 11-18, sequence part 2 and cadence

The sequence is relatively long, and variations are therefore necessary. In bar 11, the parts are redistributed, so the melodic material in the soprano is heard in the bass, and new material is heard in the soprano.

The melodic material in the bass should be a third higher; this can be seen by examining the motive in the soprano in bar 7 in the previous example, where the motive begins on the third of the D minor chord. This means, that the same motive in bar 11 should begin on the third, *d* in Bb major. However, Bach has written the entire motive a third lower. This arises a harmonic ambiguity in the sequence: the standard descending fifth sequence would have given Bb major in bar 11, em[7b5] in bar 12, and so on, while the transposed motive supports the harmony G minor in bar 11, C[9] in bar 12, an so on. (See the chords in brackets in the example).

Ex. 41, ML: Harmonic ambiguity

Such harmonic ambiguity is relatively common in Bach, especially in sequences, and is almost always found between chords/chord progressions a third from each other, (and thus have a miniumum of two common tones).

At the end of bar 14, the sequence ends, as shown by the tone *Bb*, which is tied over as a suspension in bar 15, and a cadential preparation in **Tp** is heard. Pay attention to how the descending fifth sequence is returned to its rightful place, with dm[7] in bar 14, gm on the third beat of bar 14, and C[7] in bar 15, which finally leads to F in bar 16.

Minor tonality, first section

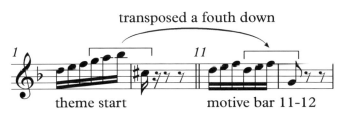

Ex. 42, Bach: Analysis, exposition: Invention no. 4 in D minor, bar 1 & 11, motivic material from the theme

Upon closer examination of the motivic material in the soprano in bar 11, it is clear that it is directly derived from the opening of the theme, as the last 4 notes of the theme are transposed a fouth down.

Thus, a higher degree of motivic concentration is acheived, making the piece even more concise.

Important points

- The second entry follows the first immediately and is an octave below

- The counterpoint makes the underlying harmony clearer, and complements the theme motivically and rhythmically

- The redundant entry is heard in a new octave. Thus, the entire movement is refreshed, and this section is given a fresh start

- The relatively long descending fifth sequence is in two sections, with a switch of voices. The melodic material is based on the material of the theme and counterpoint

- The modulation to **Tp** ends with a cadence

Analysis: Bach: Invention no. 13 in A minor, section I

This invention is in 4/4 and in a fast tempo.

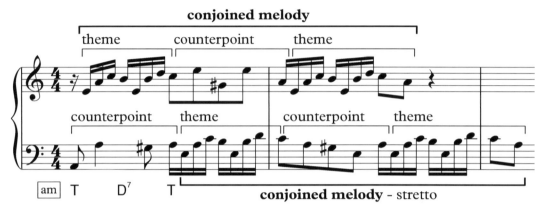

Ex. 43, Bach: Analysis, exposition: Invention no. 13 in A minor, bar 1-3, theme and counterpoint

The theme is unusually short, lasting only two beats. It comprises an arpeggiation in ♪ over the basic functions, **T** and **D**^{7}, and has a strong upward motion toward the third of the tonic on the third beat of bar 1.

A counterpoint is heard with the first entry, which is often only found in slow or very long themes. It comprises a leap of an opctave from the root, which is held as a 4-3 suspension against the dominant, and resolves to the leading tone. As such, A minor is clearly established as the tonality. The counterpoint complements the theme, both rhythmically and melodically, through the use of longer note-values and stepwise motion.

On the third beat, an answer an octave below in the bass is presented, but with a new counterpoint in ♪, which, like the previous counterpoint, complements the theme rhythmically. However, unlike the first counterpoint, this counterpoint is built upon arpeggiation instead of stepwise motion.

Conjoined melody

In bar 2, two redundant entries in the soprano and bass are heard. However, these entries are not in new octaves. This undoubtedly is due to the fact the that theme is short, and the redundant entries in each voice, together with the counterpoint, form a long conjoined melody (see ex. 43). The conjoined melody in bar 1-2 is heard, in stretto, two beats later in the bass.

For further description and work with "conjoined melody", see *volume II, Advanced techniques for working with inventions, invention with short themes.*

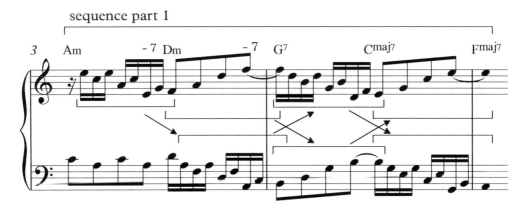

Ex. 44, Bach: Analysis, exposition: Invention no. 13 in A minor, bar 3-5, descending fifth sequence part 1

A descending fifth sequence begins in bar 3. There are two chord changes in each bar, and the motivic material is based on the arpeggiation from the theme and counterpoint.

The sequence can be described as a "cross-sequence", as the motivic material crosses between the soprano and bass with each chord change.

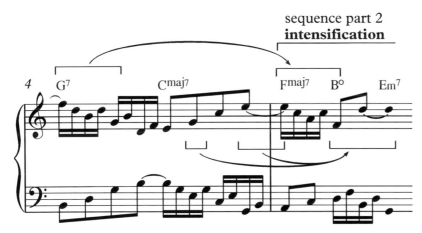

Ex. 45, Bach: Analysis, exposition: Invention no. 13 in A minor, bar 4-5½, sequence part 2, intensification

In bar 5, the sequence is accelerated, with four chord changes in every bar instead of two.

The motivic material is also intensified, as the material that previously lasted one bar, lasts only 2 beats. In practice, Bach achieves this by using appropriate motivic material from each chord in the first part of the sequence, such that it only lasts a ♩ instead of a ♩..

In this case, Bach has used the first ♩ from G⁷ in bar 4 and the leap of a sixth, that arises from using the tones *g* and *e* from C^maj7 in bar 4.

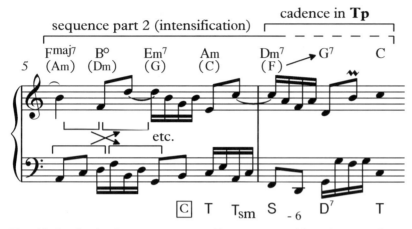

Ex. 46, Bach: Analysis, exposition: Invention no. 13 in A minor, bar 5-6½, sequence part 2 and cadence

Like the first part, the second part of the sequence can be described as a "cross-sequence". Bars 5-6½ can clearly be heard as an intensification of the descending fifth sequence, albeit with more intense harmonic rhythm.

However, like the D minor invention, it is clear that harmonic ambiguity can also be seen here, as the chords can also be interpreted as being a third higher than the chords in the sequence (see the chords in brackets).

This ambiguity is removed from bar 6, where F major (in brackets) functions as $S \rightarrow D^7$.

Rather unusually, the soprano continues the falling fifth sequence completely into the cadence, making it difficult to separate the two sections, especially in the soprano.

This sequence in built upon falling thirds, which gives many possibilities for multiple interpreations of the chords.

Falling fifth sequences built wholly or in part upon falling thirds is relatively common in Bach's music. This often results in a kind of "tonic submediant effect", as seen in the bass in this example. The D minor chord is substituted with H° enroute to G major, and the C major substituted with A minor enroute to the F major chord.

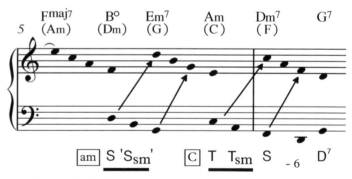

Ex. 47, Bach: Analysis, exposition: Invention no. 13 in A minor, bars 5-6½, falling thirds

Canon

The whole exposition can also be considered to be a long canon at the lower octave, in which the bass begins two beats later, in relation to the soprano. This is not a strict canon; the answer in the bass is varied, and it is also transposed a fifth in the sequence, to accomodate the falling fifth sequence. In the second part of the sequence (bar 5), the canon is continued, like the rest of the sequence, such that the bass is only one ♩ later than the soprano. The general feel of a canon is nonetheless clear, up to the cadence.

Important points

- The second entry is heard immediately after the first an octave below

- The theme, counterpoint, and redundant entry form a *complete melody*, which is intensified in the bass through the use of stretto

- The counterpoint makes the underlying harmony clear, and complements the theme both motivically and rhythmically

- Due to the short theme, redundant entries are *not* in new octaves

- A relatively long descending fifth sequence in two parts is used. Cross-sequence and intensification in the second part, based on the motivic material from the theme and coutnerpoint

- The modulation to **Tp** ends with a cadence

- This invention resembles a canon, without being a strict canon

---

Themes and the development of counterpoint

The themes of Bach's inventions can be fast or slow, and vary widely in length (see also *Volume II: Further development of the invention*). As such, it is most meaningful to work with themes that are in a relatively fast tempo and not too long; a theme of moderate length in a relatively fast tempo ensures that the length of each individual section in the form is manageable, and at the same time provides ample opportunities for harmonic richness and variation in the interpretation of the theme.

When working on a two-part invention in the style of Bach, a theme should be carefully chosen. The theme should be 1-1½ long in 4/4 and 2-3 bars in 3/8. The tempo should be relatively fast, with mainly ♪ and ♪ motion (see also *Themes for two-part invention, Appendix E*, page 118f.).

Two themes will be worked upon in this section:

Ex. 48, ML: Theme I and II, exercise in minor invention

Theme I – distribution of themes

The theme often begins in the soprano or occasionally in the bass. It is immediately answered in the other voice at a distance of an octave.

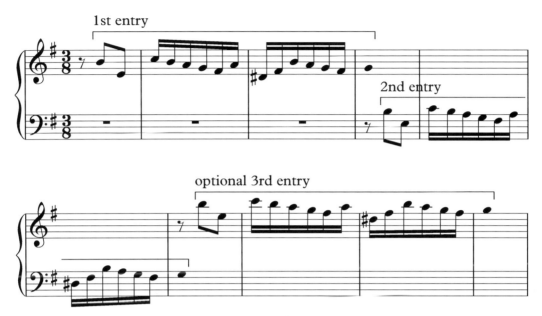

Ex. 49, ML: Theme I, placement of second and optional third entry

The third entry, if present, is often used to prepare the voices for a sequence, as seen in Invention no. 4 in D minor (*Appendix C,* page 113), which has a redundant entry in the soprano in bar 5 that lifts the voices up and allows for a long fall in the following sequence, leading to the cadence in bar 18 in F major.

Important: In 4/4, beats 1 and 3 are equally strong. Therefore, a 1½-bar long theme should be answered after 1½ bars, on the third beat of bar 2.

Counterpoint

The countermelody to the theme is called the counterpoint. The first entry of the theme is sometimes accompanied by a countermelody, mainly in the case of relatively long themes.

This volume will focus on counterpoint that begins with the second entry of the theme.

The counterpoint is worked out in three steps:

1) Find the functions/chords

The basic harmonic rhythm is ♩ in 4/4 and ♩. in 3/8 (one chord per bar). However, it is also common to harmonise with one chord per ♩ in 4/4 and two chords per bar in 3/8 (harmonic rhythm: ♩ + ♪ or ♪+ ♩). The harmony is often based upon the classical **cadence**:

Always	T		D⁽⁷⁾	T
If possible		incomplete S/S⁶		
Sometimes	Tsm			

a) Basic functions: Always start with **T** and end with **D⁽⁷⁾** leading to **T**.

b) If possible, use **S⁶** or the incomplete **S** before **D**

> **Important:** As soon as **S** can be used, write both **S⁶** and the incomplete **S** in the music, as it is crucial to have both possibilities when working on the counterpoint and sequence.

c) Sometimes, derivatives of **T** are used before **S**, such as **T Taf S⁶ D⁷ T**.

2) Central tones

Find the tones in the counterpoint, which express the underlying harmony most clearly when considered together with the theme, such as the root+third, root/third+seventh, or third+ninth. These intervals are especially important on the strong beats of the bar (first and third in 4/4 and first in 3/8).

The interval of a fifth can be used with care, as if the same counterpoint is used in the soprano instead of the bass (and vice-versa), the fifth becomes a fourth, and thus a dissonant interval (see also *Fifth of the chord in the bass* page 13).

3) Working on the counterpoint

This aspect is the most important and time-consuming. Find the functions/chords, central tones, and begin composing with the piano. When something sounds good, figure out what works (or not), and try again. Do not hesitate to start over. Write multiple versions, and finally choose the one that seems most independent and elegant, which hopefully also sounds like it was created in a moment of inspiration.

Complementary rhythm: long note-values in a voice should be accompanied by shorter note-values in the other voice, and vice-versa. Thus, there is constant ♪ motion (see also ex. 24 page 21).

To begin writing the counterpoint easily, start with the following:

- With ♪ motion in the theme, use **broken chords** in ♪ in the counterpoint

- With ♪ in the theme, use ♪ in **stepwise motion** in the counterpoint

The rhythm of the theme and counterpoint should complement each other, such that the note-values or figures used in the counterpoint are not used in the theme.

If possible, the counterpoint should have a characteristic feature, such as a special leap, a characteristic rhythm, syncopation, or motion, which makes the counterpoint independent of the theme.

Theme I in E minor

Examples in working out the counterpoint:

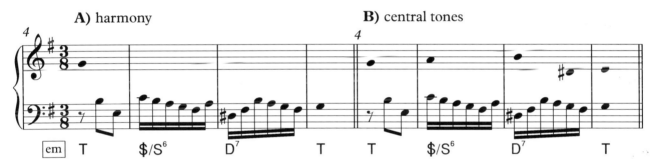

Ex. 50, ML: Theme I, harmony and central tones

A) **Suitable functions**: **T**, incomplete **S/S⁶**, **D⁽⁷⁾** and **T**.

B) **Central tones**: In the first bar (bar 4), we see a clear framing of E minor through the leap from fifth to root. The best tone in the soprano is therefore the third, which, as the last tone of the first entry, is an obvious choice.

Second bar: the ♪-motion in the theme clearly expresses an incomplete **S** (through the tones *a*, *c*, and *f#*). The third is sounded on the first beat, making the root a clear choice in the soprano. *f#* is also possible, but it lacks the clear expression of the subdominant function as the root, while the central tones, *e* and *c*, will be heard as **Tsᴵᴵᴵ** (C major).

Third bar: The root is the most obvious choice, but *f#*, *a*, and *c* (the ninth) are also possibilities, as long as any dissonances are treated correctly. In the dominant, it is crucial that the leading tone is used: if it is absent in the theme, it should be used in the counterpoint. In this example, the occasional leading tone in the counterpoint works well with the theme.

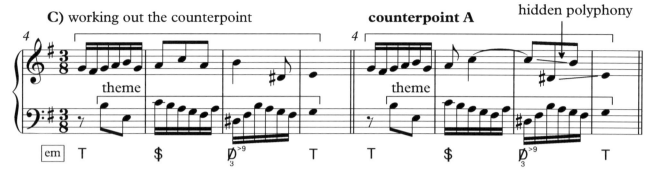

Ex. 51, ML: Theme I, working out counterpoint A

C) First bar: The use of complementary rhythm requires ♪ motion that naturally leads from the third of **T** (*g*) to the root of **S** (*a*).

Second bar: The movement from the fundamental to the third and back again works fine but is also a bit boring. Instead, in **counterpoint A** the third is used as a preparation for the suspended ninth in the next bar. This gives a new rhythmic characteristic that also functions as a suspension, thus creating forward motion in the counterpoint.

Third bar: the tied *c* is the dissonant ninth of the dominant, and must be resolved to *b*. However, *b* will not work well on the second beat, as it will form an octave with the theme. Thus, *d#* (the leading tone) is introduced on the second beat, leading to the root (*e*) in the next bar. This note of ornamentation also introduces, briefly, hidden polyphony to the counterpoint (see also *hidden polyphony* page 25f.).

Ex. 52, ML: Theme I, working out counterpoint B

Counterpoint B

If the themes are exchanged such that the second theme appears in the soprano, it is possible to use a scalic passage in ♪ motion to lead to the root of the subdominant in the second bar. On the second beat in the second and third bar, a passing tone is found, which in bar 3 can be interpreted as a ⁺**S** with the rising melodic minor passage in the bass.

Theme II in D minor

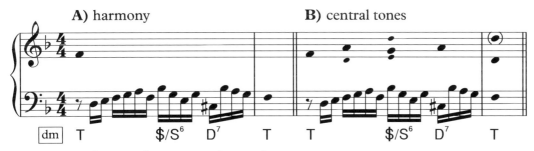

Ex. 53, ML: Theme II, harmony and central tones

This theme is relatively easy to harmonise. Pay attention to the downward-moving broken chords on the third beat, which also are the tones of the incomplete subdominant.

The first central tone, *f*, is given from the beginning, and on the second beat, the missing chord-tones *a* and possibly *d* are good choices. On the subdominant, there are many more choices: *g* is obvious, but *e*, which forms a tritone with the bass, is also an interesting choice, as the effect the of the incomplete subdominant is considerably strengthened. *d* is difficult to employ, as is the dissonant fifth of S^6 and thus needs preparation and resolution to the leading tone (see also *Harmony*, page 89 and *Suspensions* page 17).

On D^7, the leading tone is in the bass, thus, the root, *a*, is a clear choice for the central tone. Similarly, the root of the following **T** is a good choice for the central tone.

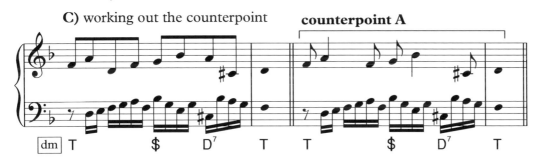

Ex. 54, ML: Theme II, development of counterpoint A

In working out the counterpoint, a first attempt with broken chords in ♪ motion is made. However, this lacks character. The prolongation of the second and sixth ♪ is relatively simple, and gives the counterpoint rhythmic potency as well as a motivic repetition that drives the music forward. A possible weakness is that fresh tones are not heard in the counterpoint: the lowest, and especially the highest tones tones are the same in the theme and the counterpoint, and a higher tone (such as *d*) could be used effectively.

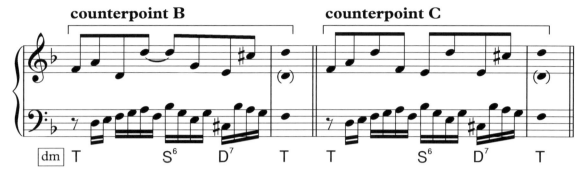

Ex. 55, ML: Theme II, counterpoint B and C

In **counterpoint B**, the highest tone, *d*, is tied over in **S⁶** on the third beat, and thus prepares for the dissonant fifth in **S⁶**. Pay attention to the resolution to the leading tone, which naturally cannot come on the fourth beat, and is therefore delayed with a few notes of ornamentation. Thus, hidden polyphony is also present here, as in ex. 33, page 25.

Ex. 56, ML: Theme II, hidden polyphony, counterpoint B

Counterpoint C is built upon the same principles, but notes of ornamentation are used between the preparation and dissonance, and between the dissonance and resolution. The character resembles a cadence even more, and the counterpoint is perhaps slightly weaker than counterpoint B, due to *d*, the highest tone, being repeated three times.

Sequence: first half

The method of writing a sequence can be divided into two parts:

1. The first half: use of **motivic material from the theme**

2. the second half: **Variation** of the sequence

The entries of the theme are normally followed by a longer section that modulates to **Tp**, often through the use of a sequence.

Basic characteristics of a sequence

In a sequence, the motivic material and chords are repeated, but shifted a certain interval (for example, a second down). Each repetition in a sequence is called a segment, and a sequence should be described by indicating:

1. How long each segment is

2. How far and in which direction the segments are shifted with every repetition

3. Which harmony is used in the sequence

In the following examples, a relatively long descending fifth sequence with about four to five segments is used. As Bach normally uses a maximum of three similar segments in a sequence, the sequence should be varied and thus can naturally be divided into two halves.

This sequence is derived from Bach's Invention in D minor, bars 7-15 (*Appendix C, all examples*, page 113) and A minor bars 3-6 (page 114).

Important: The harmonic rhythm is ♩ in 4/4 and ♩. in 3/8:

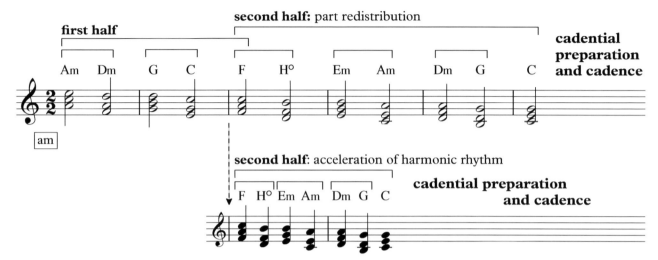

Ex. 57, ML: Chords in the descending fifth sequence

The chords can also be found in *Appendix B, sequences,* page 98

Descending fifths

One of the most important sources of coherence in Bach's music is the motivic concentration, as seen in his inventions and fugues, where the motivic material of the whole piece is often exclusively derived from the theme and counterpoint.

Using *Theme I* and *II*, a method will be presented, which can be used to find suitable motivic material from the theme, to be used in the first half of the descending fifths sequence.

Descending fifths: Theme I in E minor

1) Find suitable motivic material from the theme and/or counterpoint.

Method:

*The motivic material from a theme that harmonically moves from **T** to **S** or from **D** to **T** in two beats (4/4) or a whole bar (3/8) can be used directly to create a descending fifth sequence.*

The distance between the chords in the sequence is always a descending fifth. There are two chords per bar (one a bar in 3/8), and the harmonic rhythm is therefore ♩ i 4/4 and ♩. in 3/8, as mentioned.

Therefore, the motivic material should be able to harmonically move a fifth downwards over the course of two beats (whole bar in 3/8).

Main functions: descending fifth in two beats (4/4) or a whole bar (3/8):

descending fifth			
T	→	**S**	typical in the beginning of the theme
D	→	**T**	typical in the ending of the theme

In *Theme I*, we can find a descending fifth from **T** to **S** and from **D** to **T**. Therefore:

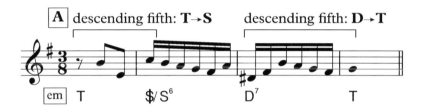

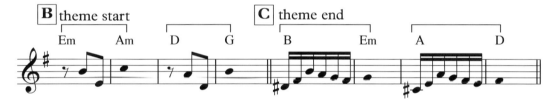

Ex. 58, ML: Theme I, sequence of the thematic material

A) In this theme, **T** leads to **S** and **D**[7] leads to **T** in the course of a bar, and the motivic material can thus be used directly in the descending fifth sequence (see **B** and **C**).

2) **Placement of the chosen motivic material:**
   The material can either be placed on the first or second chord in the sequence, and either in the bass or the soprano. This gives four possibilities. The first chord is often used if the motivic material is from the beginning of the theme, and the second chord is used if the material is from the end. After placing the material, new material is composed to the remaining chord.

3) Working out the sequence:

   Important: If possible, use a dissonant seventh or ninth in the sequence, preferably prepared in the previous chord and tied over as a suspension. In the descending fifth sequence, the third is often tied, as this tone becomes the seventh of the chord a fifth below. The fifth can also be tied over, and it thus becomes the ninth of the next chord.

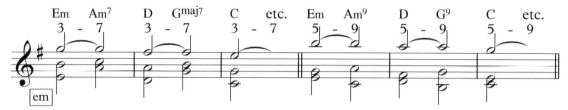

Ex. 59, ML: Treatment of dissonance, seventh and ninth

Theme I – working out the first half of the sequence

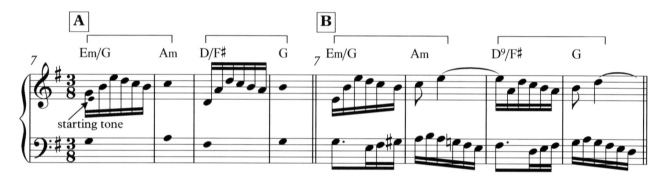

Ex. 60, ML: Theme I, working out the sequence: first half

A) In this sequence, the ending of theme (**C**) from ex. 58 Page 45 is used:

    The motive has been transposed to fit the underlying harmony **T** and is placed in the soprano.

    The very first note of the first segment is often different from the first notes of the following segments. This is due to the fact that the first segment is often connected to the previous music, in this case, the closing notes of the theme and counterpoint. Thus, the starting tone in the soprano in bar 7 is *e*, not *g*, as the previous entry of the theme in bar 5-7 ends on the root (see ex. 51 page 40).

    In 3/8, the sequence falls every other bar, making every segment two bars long. Thus, the motive is repeated after two bars, but a second below, thus sounding the harmony: D major to G major instead of E minor to A minor.

B) **The soprano**
    As mentioned, the starting tone, *e*, in the soprano in the the first bar of the sequence (bar 7) is given, as is the *g* in the bass.

Minor tonality, first section

In the next bar, the fifth of A minor works well as a tied suspension, becoming the ninth of D major through the syncopated rhythm of the counterpoint in bar 5. The ninth is resolved on the second beat of the third bar.

The bass

In the bass (bar 7), the motion from *g* to *a* is decorated with a *g#*, which is a 'dominantisation'[2] of the E minor chord towards the A minor chord, thus making the E minor chord a temporary secondary dominant in A minor. In bar 8, ♪ motion in the bass is used as a complementary rhythm to the syncopation in the soprano.

Pay attention to the resolution of *g#* in bar 8: it is important that extra accidentals in the sequence are only used to colour the sequence; the main modulation from **T** to **Tp** should not be disturbed.

---

2   Dominantisation refers to the process where a chord, typically the tonic, is modified to become a major chord with an added minor seventh, and thus becomes a (temporary) dominant. It is the opposite of 'tonicisation' where a non-tonic chord becomes a new tonic, temporarily or for a longer period of time (modulation).

Theme II – working out the first half of the sequence

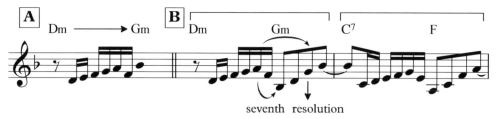

Ex. 61, ML: Theme II, material for the sequence

A) The beginning of the theme leads from **T** to **S** over the course og two beats, and thus can be used directly in the sequence.

B) The b^b on the third beat is shifted an octave down and followed by a G minor arpeggio in ♪. Pay attention to the effect of shifting the b^b down; melodically, a seventh arises between the *a* and the low b^b, and the *a* is resolved downwards to *g*.

The third in the G minor chord on the last ♪ is tied over as the seventh of C⁷ and resolved downwards to the third in the F major chord on the last ♪ of the example.

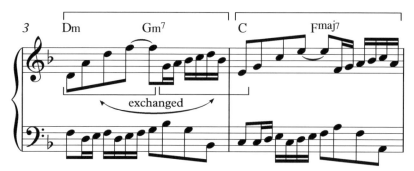

Ex. 62, ML: Theme II, working out the sequence: first half

The motive and the harmony from the previous example is exchanged. Thus, the motivic material uses a G minor chord instead of D minor. As such, the soprano is raised a fifth, has some fresh tones and space is created for a longer fall towards the coming cadence in **Tp**.

In the bass, contrary motion is used, and the ♪ motion in the soprano is complemented by using ♪ in the bass, and vice-versa.

Minor tonality, first section

The structure of the theme as material

If the motivic material from the theme cannot be used directly in the descending fifth sequence, small changes can be made to adapt the theme to suit a sequence.

A good method to finde material is to consider the theme as being comprised of different structures, such as stepwise motion and arpeggios, instead of individual tones.

Theme II – the structure of the theme as material

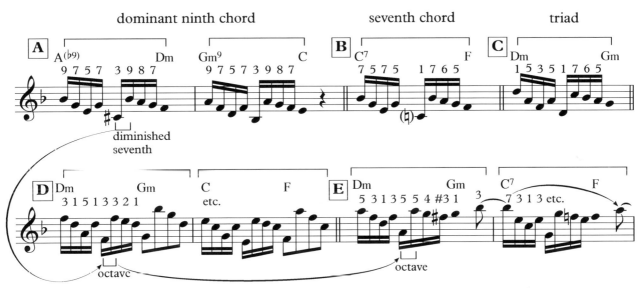

Ex. 63, ML: Theme II, the structure of the theme as material for a sequence

A) The broken chords in the ending of *Theme II* are not suited to be used directly in a sequence. The problem arises in the second segment, Gm^9 to Dm, where the broken chord outlining a major ninth and passing through the seventh does not suit the style of Bach. Generally, broken chords that include the ninth should be avoided, as these chord extensions are considered to be too drastic for the style of Bach[3]. Naturally, there are exceptions, such as the A^{b9} arpeggiation from the ninth down to the major third in the first bar of the example, which works well due to the chords clear dominant function.

B) Consider the motive structurally instead of as individual "fixed" notes:
Structure: A downward broken chord in a zigzag motion followed by an upward leap to the start tone and downward stepwise motion. In other words, a broken chord followed by

---

3   In jazz, chords are built up in thirds from the root, and *extended chords* refer to chords with the eleventh and thirteenth. Interestingly, with the development of jazz, melodies have gradually moved higher and higher up in the chord. In early jazz, the melody was often based upon the seventh and ninth of the chord, but has been gradually moved to the ninth, eleventh, and thirteenth.

stepwise motion.

By starting the broken chord on the seventh instead of the ninth, a seventh chord (C^7) is formed, which leads to F, and thus creating a figure that remarkably suits the style of Bach.

C) The root is used as the starting tone instead of the seventh, but the seventh can also be used, as long as it is prepared.

D) **The pattern placed in the descending fifth sequence**

When the ending of the theme is seen as a pattern instead of a broken chord, many new possibilities are available. The pattern, in principle, does not depend on where it begins. Thus, it can begin on the root of the chord as in (**C**), on the third (**D**), or on the fifth (**E**). In (**D**), it works well to leap down to the root, *g*, on the third beat, thus creating the same melodic effect as in ex. 61 page 48 The third of D minor, *f*, thus resolves down to the third of C major, *e*.

When a pattern is used instead of individual tones to generate the motivic material for the sequence, a small change in the character of the original motive cannot be avoided. For example, in (**D**) and (**E**), where the characteristic leap of a diminished seventh in the broken chord is changed to a more neutral octave leap.

E) Starting on the fifth of the chord.

Here, the seventh of the chord is tied over and resolved on the last ♪ of the bar.

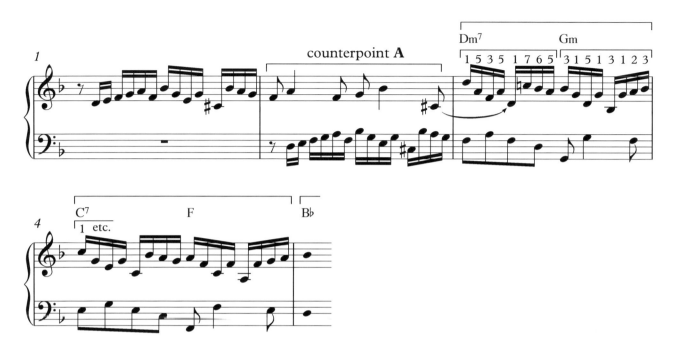

Ex. 64, ML: Theme II, working out an alternative sequence: first half

Working out the sequence, based on (**C**) and (**D**) from the previous example:

1. **Dm⁷** (bar 3, first beat): Broken chord from the root downwards, (**C**) from ex. 63 page 49:

2. **Gm** (bar 3, third beat): Broken chord from the third downwards, (**D**) from ex. 63 page 49:

As *d* is the highest tone in the sequence, **counterpoint A** is chosen (ex. 54 page 41), as counterpoint B and C (ex. 55, page 42) both have the same *d* as the highest tone.

Pay attention to the upward leap from the leading tone to the root on the last ♪ in bar 2. It adds abruptness and thus character to the start of the sequence. Melodically, the leading tone is resolved on the second beat of bar 3.

Sequence: second half

In the second half of the sequence, the material from the first half is varied.

Two effective methods:

1) Part redistribution

2) Acceleration of harmonic rhythm

Part redistribution

Based on Bach's Invention no. 4 in D minor bar 11-14, material can be redistributed from the soprano to the bass (or vice-versa), and new motivic material found for the other voice (see also analysis of Bach, Invention in D minor, ex. 40, page 30).

Important: It is typically the soprano that is redistributed to the bass, but the reverse is also possible.

Theme II – working out the sequence, second half, part redistribution

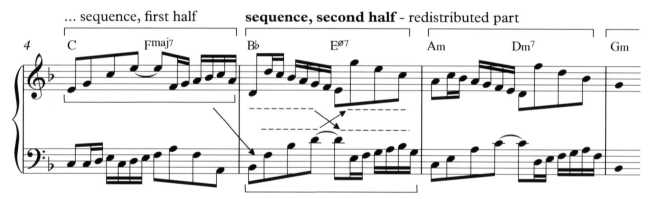

Ex. 65, ML: Theme II, sequence, second half, redistributed part

Using the sequence from ex. 62 page 48, the soprano in bar 4 is redistributed to the bass in bar 5, and a new top voice is written.

As seen in the example, the second half of the sequence (from bar 5) can be viewed as a "cross-sequence", where the motivic material in the first half of the bar is mirrored and redistributed in the next half of the bar, such that a mirrored version of the motive in the soprano is heard in the bass, and vice-versa.

Theme I – working out the sequence, second half, part redistribution

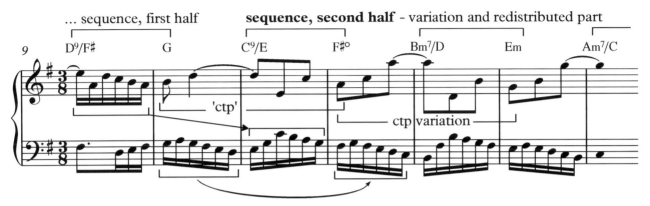

Ex. 66, ML: Theme I, sequence, second half - variation and part redistribution

Using the sequence from ex. 60 (**B**) page 46, the motive of the soprano in bar 9 is redistributed to the bass in bar 11, and a new top voice is composed, based on the last part of the counterpoint.

Bar 10 continues unchanged, and a small but important variation is found in the soprano in bar 12, which lifts the whole movement and gives fresh tones in the soprano, that have not been heard in the piece.

The soprano in bars 10-11 is the same as the last two bars of the counterpoint. These bars are repeated with a small variation in the next two bars as part of the sequence, and thus support the sense of renewal from bar 11 onwards.

Acceleration of harmonic rhythm

A common technique in the music of Bach is the acceleration of a sequence to vary and intensify. Based on Bach's Invention no. 13 in A minor, the second half of the sequence is worked out with the chord changes at double-tempo: one chord change per ♩ in 4/4 and two chord changes per bar in 3/8. This technique is best suited to 4/4, but can also be used in 3/8 (see also analysis of Bach: Invention in A minor page 33-34, ex. 45-47).

Theme II – working out the sequence, second half, acceleration of harmonic rhythm

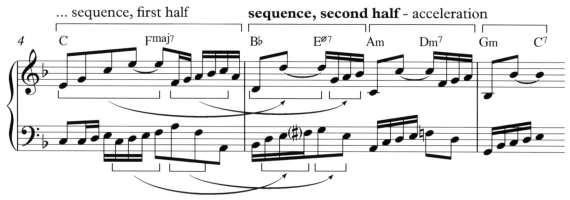

Ex. 67, ML: Theme II, sequence, second half, acceleration

The acceleration is based on the sequence from ex. 62 page 48.

In bar 5, the arpeggio in ♪ in the soprano is reduced to a leap of an octave, and the ♪ motion on beats 3 and 4 are reduced to a single beat. The ♪ and ♪ material in the bass is reduced in a similar manner.

Important: The suspension from the first half of the sequence is preserved in the accelerated version.

Pay attention to the possibility of placing a temporary leading tone, *f#*, in the upward moving passage in the bass, bar 7. This gives a short hint of a G minor chord instead of Em7♭5, and is an effect commonly seen in the music of Bach, as previously mentioned:

Harmonic ambiguity of chords a third above or below the actual chords in a descending fifth sequence.

See also the analyses of Bach: Invention no. 4 in D minor, bar 11-14 ex. 40, page 30 and Bach: Invention no. 13 in A minor, bar 5-6 ex. 46, page 34.

Theme I – working out the sequence, second half, acceleration of harmonic rhythm

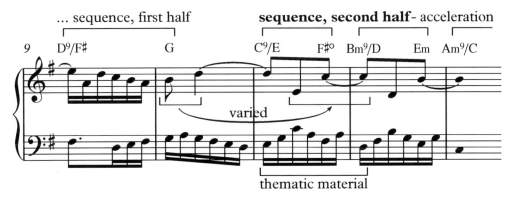

Ex. 68, ML: Theme I, sequence, second half – variation and acceleration

Variation and acceleration, based on the sequence from ex. 60 (**B**) page 46.

As mentioned, it is more difficult to accelerate the sequence in 3/8 with chord changes in double-tempo, as it results in two chords in a bar, and one of the chords must be sounded in the space of just one ♪.

In this example, this is resolved by adapting the motivic material from the theme and placing it in the bass in bar 11, together with the last section of the original counterpoint in the soprano. The thematic material in bar 11 comprises the beginning of the third bar and the ending of the second bar of the theme.

As in the previous example, the suspension from the first half of the sequence is preserved in the accelerated version.

Theme II – alternative sequence, acceleration of harmonic rhythm

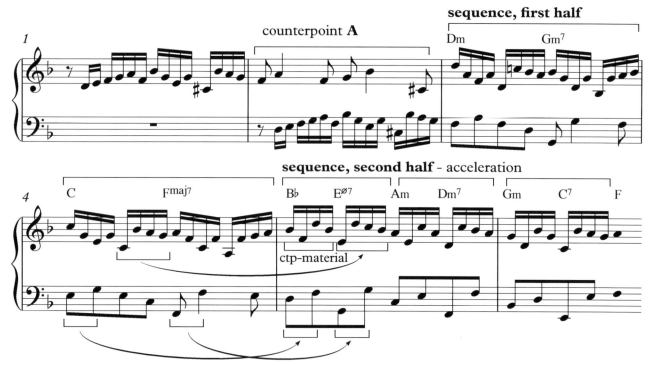

Ex. 69, ML: Theme II, alternative sequence, second half – acceleration

The acceleration of the alternative sequence from ex. 64 page 51 is carried out over the broken chords from the ending of *Theme II*. The figure on the first beat of bar 5 is altered, so it serves as preparation for the seventh on the second beat.

Pay attention to the resemblence to the counterpoint in bar 2:

Ex. 70, ML: Theme II, alternative sequence – resemblance to counterpoint

By isolating the first, third, and eighth ♪ from (**A**), the syncopated motive in (**B**) is produced, thus creating a clear connection to the counterpoint.

Cadence

In Baroque music, cadences are milestones that serve to anchor the free-floating net of voices. The cadence defines the tonality, and often closes both short and long passages in the relevant tonality. There are many cadence forms, all of which have been standardised and are seldom altered. They can therefore be lifted freely from Bach and used in the exercises.

Important: Before the cadence, a short cadential preparation lasting two beats to a bar should be included, which leads from the sequence to the cadence itself. Begin by composing a top voice, which naturally leads to the cadence.

The following is a selection of cadences from Bach's inventions, which can be freely used:

Cadences in 4/4

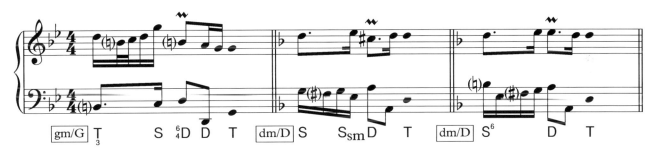

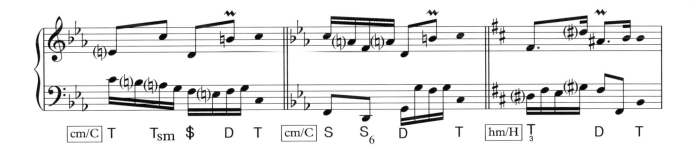

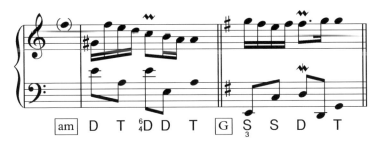

Ex. 71, Bach: Two-part cadences in 4/4

Cadences in 3/8

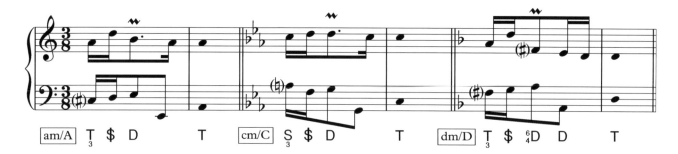

Ex. 72, Bach: Two-part cadences in 3/8

Pay attention to the leap of an octave in the bass on the dominant, which can be found in almost all cadences, This adds emphasis to the cadence, as well as the open fifths that arise when the soprano has the fifth in the final **D** chord before **T**.

Minor tonality, first section

Cadential preparation and cadence

Theme II – cadential preparation and cadence

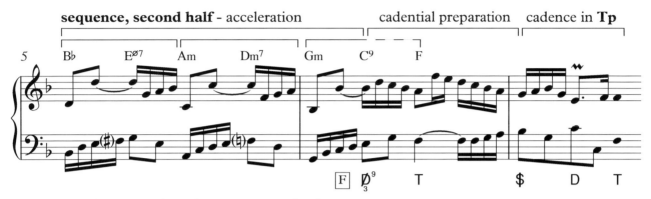

Ex. 73, ML: Theme II, cadential preparation and cadence

After a long descending fifth sequence, a small upward motion in the soprano is effective in giving the music energy before it settles down in the cadence, almost like a small 'aftermath' of the long descending course of the sequence, thus energising the music and making the following cadence sound more stable.

In the example above, the previous accelerated descending fifth sequence ex. 67 page 54 ends in the third segment (bar 6) with a small variation of the dominant chord C^9, which leads to the tonic, F. In the following transition, the soprano leaps upwards, only to fall to rest in the cadence.

Theme I – cadential preparation and cadence

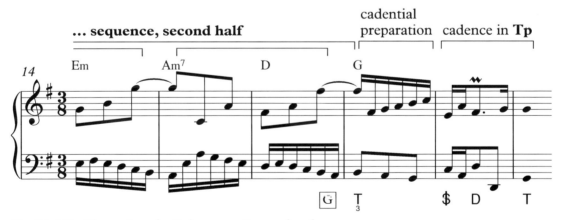

Ex. 74, ML: Theme I, cadential preparation and cadence

This example develops ex. 66 page 53 further. The movement is already lifted up in the soprano through the course of the sequence, and thus, a downward-moving figure is more suitable leading to the cadence in bar 18. See also *Appendix C, all examples* page 102-112.

Alternative solutions

Naturally, there are alternative solutions to be found when writing the first section of a minor invention. The most common are:

1. Answering at the fifth

2. Episode without descending fifth sequence

3. Canon

4. Modulation to other tonalities than **Tp**

Answering at the fifth

Ex. 75, ML: Theme I, answering at the fifth

Based upon Bach's Invention no. 15 in B minor.

When answering at the fifth, the theme should be modified slightly, as the first entry ends on **T** in E minor, and the second entry thus begins on **S** in the dominant tonality, B minor (ex. 75, bar 4). This modification of the start of the theme in the second entry is known as a *tonal answer*, as the change is brought about because of the tonality, as opposed to a *real answer*, which is an answer without any modifications.

Often, only one or two tones in the theme are changed; in this theme, the first tone is changed from *f#* to *e*, so as to remain in the underlying E minor harmony.

A common rule-of-thumb for tonal answers is:

If the root or the fifth is emphasised at the beginning of the theme, the root should be answered with the fifth from the original tonality, and the fifth should be answered with the root from the original tonality.

The theme leaps from fifth to root in bar 1, and thus is answered in bar 4 with a leap from the root to the fifth from the original tonality, E minor.

In these short two-part inventions with answers at the fifth, the music typically stays in the dominant tonality to establish a tonal centre before modulating towards **Tp**. This is achieved through a redundant entry in B minor in bar 7 with a *real answer* instead of the tonal answer from bar 4.

The sequence in bars 10-15 is relatively short; it is harmonically simple, without seventh or ninth suspensions, but with submediant derivations every other chord (in brackets). The sequence is in 3 segments, and is motivically based on the middle part of the theme (bar 2).

Pay attention to the cadential preparation in bar 16, where the $F^{\#o}$ chord gets a *d* in the bass, and thus becomes a **D⁷** for the new tonic in G major. The alteration of a diminished chord to form a dominant seventh chord will be seen again under *Short sequences in major inventions* (page 77f).

Episode without descending fifth sequence

As an alternative to using the descending fifth sequence in the first episode, Bach occasionally uses the stepwise ascending sequence (Rosalia sequence)[4], the sequence ascending by thirds, a descending sequence/pattern by thirds, or an episode without a sequence.[5]

Alternatives to Tp

Often, the parallel tonality is visited so some extent after the first section. However, **Tp** is sometimes replaced with a direct modulation to **D**. For example, refer to the slow Invention no. 9 in F minor by Bach.

Canon

Canon is a technique occasionally used by Bach, for example in Invention no. 2 in C minor and no. 8 in F major and partly in no. 13 in A minor (see also *Appendix D, Bach invention, 1st section* page 114 and 116). In terms of the form, a canon has a significant effect on the movement. In invention no. 2 in C minor, the music moves directly to **Tp** after the second entry before starting a descending fifth sequence above the counterpoint to the original theme.

For a more exhaustive examination of the use of canon in inventions, refer to the section on canons under major invention (page 81f).

4　See also *volume II*, working with the invention, completing the exposition, *Theme IV*
5　Bach uses the stepwise falling sequence (fifth sequence) in the first episode in more than half of his inventions (9 out of 16). Alternatives for the first episode are:
- Stepwise ascending sequence (Rosalia sequence): Invention no. 5
- Pattern ascending by thirds: Invention no. 11
- Pattern/sequence descending by thirds: Invention no. 1 and 8
- No sequence: Invention no. 3 (with dominant pedal point) and no. 9 (variations on the theme)

Major invention, section I

The themes that will be worked on will be, like with the minor inventions, instrumental, and thus relatively fast themes, which last 1-1½ beats in 4/4 and 2-3 beats in 3/8.

The major invention modulates to the **D** instead of **Tp** tonality, but other than this, functions in the same manner as the minor invention, with one important difference: the beginning of the sequence (see also *Sequence: first half* page 71f):

Analysis: Bach: Invention no. 6 in E major, section I

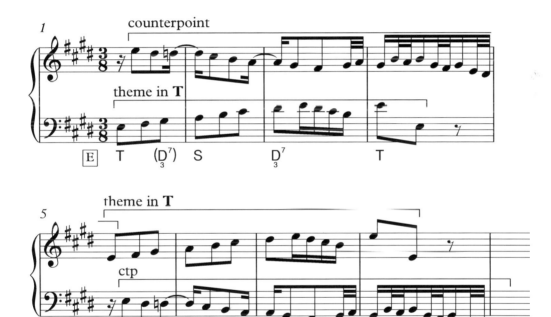

Ex. 76, Bach: Analysis: Invention no. 6 in E major, bars 1-9, theme and counterpoint

The invention is in 3/8 and in a calmer tempo.

The theme is 4 bars long, and comprises a long rising movement up to bar 4, where the leap of an octave finally leads back to the starting tone, *e*. The rhythm is in regular ♪, with the exception of a turn in ♫ leading to the top tone, *e*, in bar 4.

As the theme is relatively long, the counterpoint is already heard when the first entry begins. The counterpoint is an *obligate counterpoint*[6], as it is always the same, or almost the same, when the theme appears. It is in perfect balance with the theme, with regular syncopated ♪ in contrary motion, and is resolved rhythmically with a ♪ pattern: ♫ in the ending of bar 3. This pattern, which will be used extensively in the rest of the movement, is motivically based on a broken chord with turns in ♬ around the individual notes in the chord.

Pay attention to the harmonic interval of a fourth on the second beat of bar 8. The use of a chord with its fifth in the bass on a relatively strong beat of the bar is quite uncommon, especially with a slower tempo, as in this invention. However, this is acceptable in this case, as the fifth in the bass is part of an arpeggio (see also *Fifth of the chord in the bass*, page 13).

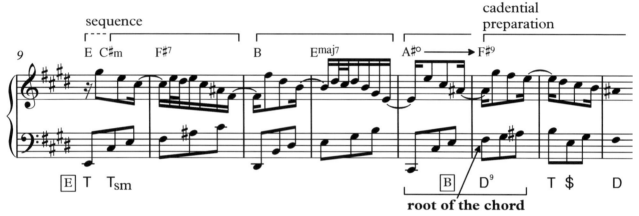

Ex. 77, Bach: Analysis: Invention no. 6 in E major, bar 9-16, sequence and cadential preparation

In bar 9, the rhythm from the first bars of the theme is combined with the arpeggiation of the counterpoint in bar 4. Motivically, it uses a descending fifth sequence, starting from **Tsm** (C#m), which is a commonly used technique in major (see also page 71f).

The sequence is relatively short, and is left in bar 14 by adding an extra tone in the bass. The chord A#° becomes F#[7], and thus becoming the function **D**[7(9)] in B major.

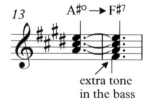

Ex. 78, ML: Analysis, bars 13-14

This compositional technique will later be used as the starting point for a method for creating a short sequence that leads to the **D** tonality. (see also *Short seqence with harmonic ambiguity*, page 77, and *Major-invention – first section*, page 100).

---

6 In some of Bach's fugues/inventions, he uses an identical or almost identical counterpoint for all entries in the movement. This is known as *obligate* counterpoint, as opposed to *free* counterpoint, where the counterpoint varies through the movement.

Major invention, section I

Ex. 79, Bach: Analysis: Invention nr. 6 in E major, bar 16-20, cadence and coda

As a counterweight to the relatively short sequence and modulation to **D**, a longer section follows with a harmonic progression in bars 15-16, a cadence in bar 17, and a short coda on the **T** chord in bars 18-20.

Important elements

- Relatively long theme and counterpoint as countermelody as soon as the first entry

- Obligate counterpoint

- Second entry of the theme begins immediately after the first at an octave

- The counterpoint makes the underlying harmony clear in the theme and complements both the motive and rhythm of the theme

- Short descending fifth sequence started on the **Tsm** and based on the motivic material from the theme and counterpoint

- Modulation to **D** ends with a slightly longer cadential preparation, cadence, and coda

---

Analysis: Bach: Invention no. 8 in F major, section I

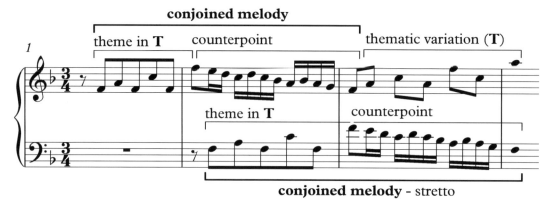

Ex. 80, Bach: Analysis: Invention no. 8 in F major, bars 1-4, theme and counterpoint

The theme is short, and like Bach's Invention no. 13 in A minor, it is closely connected with the counterpoint in a long melodic passage. If the theme and counterpoint is considered as a single conjoined melody lasting two bars, then the use of stretto in bar 2 is apparent. This is as the melody of the bass begins before the soprano has completed its melody, and thus, they overlap each other by a bar (see also analysis of Bach: Invention no. 13 in A minor page 32).

The theme (bar 1) is one bar long, and comprises a bouncing F major broken chord in ♪ from the root to the same note an octave above. This tension is released in the counterpoint (bar 2) through a turning scalewise motion in ♪ leading back to the root. In bar 3, a varied version of the theme is heard in the soprano, which, together with the counterpoint in the bass, leads to a short transition to C major.

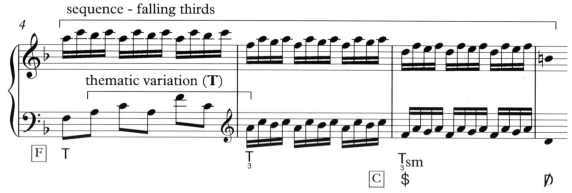

Ex. 81, Bach: Analysis: Invention no. 8 in F major, bar 4-7, pattern in falling thirds

The short transition introduces a new bouncing ♪ figure (soprano, bar 4), which is imitated in the bass and descends by thirds.

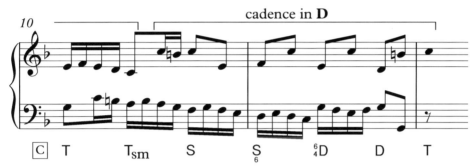

Ex. 82, Bach: Analysis: Invention no. 8 in F major, bar 7-12, cadential preparation and cadence

After the modulation to **D**, a cadential preparation based on the motivic material from the theme and counterpoint is heard. It leads to a longer closing cadence in **D**.

Canon

The entire exposition is a characterised by the use of a canon in the lower octave (bar 1-11), with almost strict imitation in the bass at the distance of a bar. It lasts up to the second beat in bar 11 with few changes, which are brought about as a result of the modulation to **D** (soprano, bar 7, as compared to bass, bar 8).

The strict canon technique has important structural significance. Aside from other aspects, it forces the use of a sequence in descending thirds (bars 4-7 ex. 81), instead of a descending fifth sequence or other ascending or descending *scalewise* sequences. Naturally, there are other possibilities, but the use of an ascending or descending scalewise sequence is especially difficult when working with a two-part canon at the octave.

Important elements

- Second entry of the theme begins immediately after the first at an octave

- The theme and counterpoint form a *complete melody*, which is intensified in the bass through the use of stretto

- The counterpoint makes the underlying harmony clear in the theme and complements both the motive and rhythm of the theme

- **Canon** as a guiding principle

- Transition based on motivic material from the theme and counterpoint in a descending third pattern, due to the strict canon principle

- Modulation to **D** ends with a cadence

Themes and the development of counterpoint

In this section, two major tonality themes will be worked upon:

Ex. 83, ML: Theme III and IV to be worked on to create an invention

Theme III

The same method is used as with the minor invention:

Ex. 84, ML: Theme III, harmony and central tones

A) Functions: The theme can easily be harmonised with a tonal cadence, with **Tsm** leading to the incomplete **S**

B) Central tones: Pay attention at **Tsm**, which is heard only on the fourth quaver beat. This is to avoid a bare fifth on the relatively strong beat.

C) working out the counterpoint

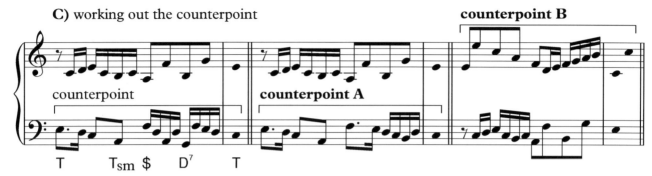

Ex. 85, ML: Theme III, working out the counterpoint

C) The third between the first two central tones is filled out with stepwise motion, and the central tones on the second beat are sounded in ♪. This is followed by broken chords in ♪ on the third and fourth beat. This is effective, but **counterpoint A** is better, because of the sequence between the first two and last two beats.

In **counterpoint B**, the voices are exchanged to allow the counterpoint to reach higher. Pay attention to the last upward ♪ motion, which should lead to the high *c*, but is slightly delayed, so the low *c* can be heard as part of a stepwise passage from *e* on the first beat, to *d* on the second quaver of the third beat to *c* in the next bar. This passage in the counterpoint creates hidden polyphony, as mentioned earlier (see also page 25f).

Theme IV

Ex. 86, ML: Theme IV, working out the counterpoint

In this theme, which exclusively uses ♪ motion, a counterpoint based on broken chords in ♪ motion is created. The counterpoint is also developed through sequence, like **counterpoint A** from the previous theme.

Sequence: first half

The major invention, as mentioned, modulates to **D**. In many cases, in order to create a natural modulation to **D**, the descending fifth sequence begins on **Tsm** instead of **T** (see also *Appendix B, sequences* page 98f). As with the minor invention, the sequence is divided into two halves.

Method

The beginning of the sequence is harmonically special, as it uses a derivation of **T: Tsm**. Thus, an effective method is to start by forming the 2nd segment in the sequence **before** using this to create the 1st segment.

As with the minor invention, suitable motivic material is found from within the theme or counterpoint.

Theme III

Ex. 87, ML: Theme III, sequence, first half - motivic material

A) The chords of the first bars of the sequence are written down. The harmony of *Theme III* leads naturally from **T** to **S** through the course of two beats, and using the opening of the theme in the descending fifth sequence is thus a clear choice.

   Important: The derivation of the tonic chord, C major, is the A minor chord on the second ♩, and the descending fifths proceed from there, starting from **Tsm**.

   The motivic material is placed in the second bar of the sequence, and it is transposed a fourth down, so that is fits in the harmony: G major to C major. Following this, a countermelody is sketched out, which, in this example, has a tied fifth from the G major to the ninth in C major.

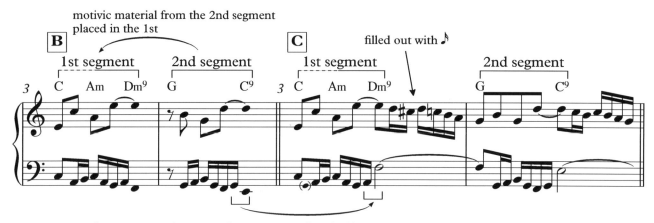

Ex. 88, ML: Theme III, working out the sequence: first half

B) The tones in the second bar of the sequence are shifted a second upward and placed in the first bar of the sequence. However, the first notes in the bass and soprano are left unchanged, as they are part of the theme and counterpoint.

C) If necessary, the tones can be altered slightly, so the first ♩ shows the derivation of **Taf** from **T**. In this example, a *g* is inserted on the second ♪ in the bass in order to retain the C major chord until the second beat. The sequence is then completed. Pay attention to use of an upward leap of a sixth instead of the original downward third leap on the third beat of the bass. This gives the music character, and also helps to emphasise the tied third, which becomes the seventh of the following G major chord.

Theme III – Alternative sequence with counterpoint B (ex. 85 page 70):

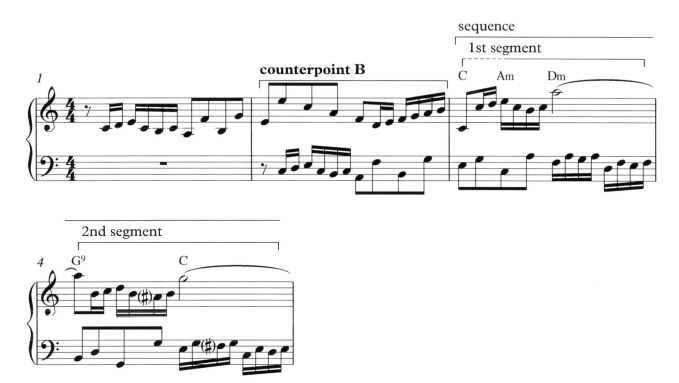

Ex. 89, ML: Theme III, working out an alternative sequence: first half

As the beginning of the theme can be harmonised with C major and A minor on the first two ♩ beats, it is also possible to use the opening directly in the sequence, without transposing it a third down, as in the previous example. Thus, the beginning of the sequence sounds like a redundant entry in the soprano, and **counterpoint B** (ex. 85 page 70) is used to reach the high register.

Important: because bar 3 sounds like a redundant entry in the soprano, it is important that the first and second entries are in the soprano and bass respectively, such that the "third"entry is an *octave* higher than the first entry in the soprano, and thus fresh and not too close to the earlier entry in the soprano.

Theme IV

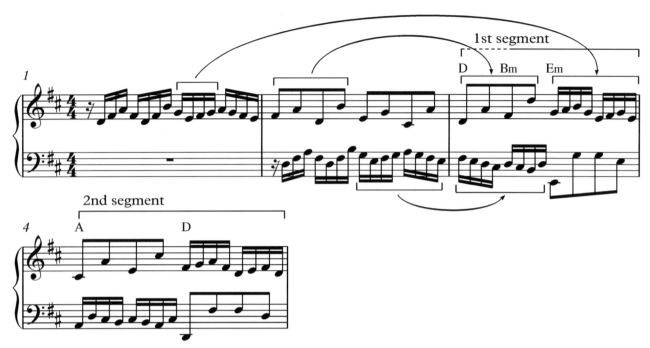

Ex. 90, ML: Theme IV, working out the sequence: first half

In this sequence, the motivic material from the theme and counterpoint is used more indirectly. This is especialy so for the figure on the third ♩ in the theme, which is used on multiple occasions in the sequence in inversion and retrograde.

Major invention, section I

Sequence: second half

In major tonality, there are two basic options when working out a descending fifth sequence that leads to a cadence in the **D** tonality.

1. Long version, similar to the descending fifth sequence in minor

2. Short version, directly modulating to **D**

Long sequence with variation in the second half

Based on: Bach: Invention no. 12 in A major bar 5-8, although the modutation is to til **Tp** instead of **D** (*Appendix D, Bach invention, 1st section*, page 117).

The long version is similar to the sequence in minor invention, except that the starting point of the sequence is **Tsm** instead of **T** (see also *Appendix B, sequences*, long sequence in major, page 100f).

Theme III

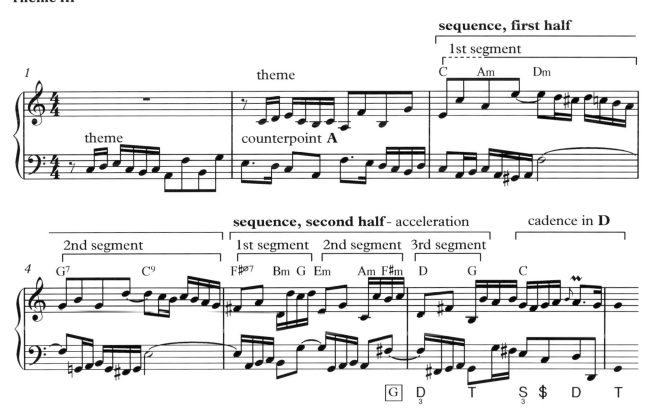

Ex. 91, ML: Theme III, sequence – long version

As mentioned, the first part is worked out from **Tsm** (ex. 88-89, page 72-73). The sequence remains in the **T** tonality until the beginning of the second half in bar 5, where the *f#* is included as a fixed element in the harmonic sequence, thus naturally modulating to the **D** tonality.

The second half of the sequence is varied according to the same principles as in minor tonality. In this example, the acceleration of the original sequence in bar 5 is an obvious choice, but it would also be possible to use part redistribution and variation, as in the minor invention.

Alternativ sekvens: *Theme III* (ex. 89, page 73):

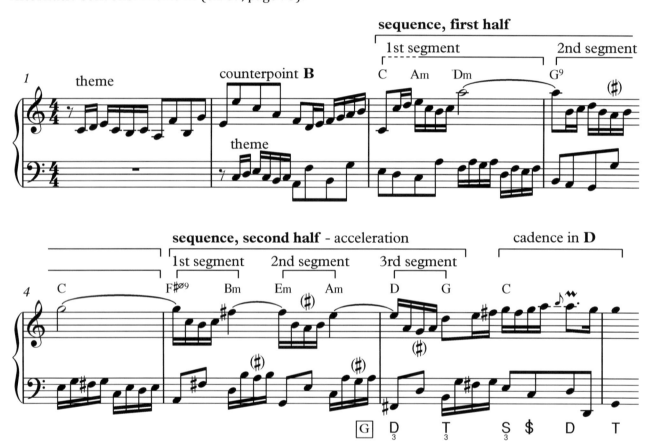

Ex. 92, ML: Theme III, alternative sequence – long version

As in the previous example, the original material in the sequence is accelerated in the second half of bar 5. Pay attention to the possibility of using neighbour leading tones (accidentals in brackets); these are local neighbour tones and thus do not influence the general harmony.

Short seqence with harmonic ambiguity

Based on: Bach: Invention no. 6 in E major, bars 9-20 (see also *Appendix D, Bach invention, 1st section,* page 115).

The short sequence has only 2½ segments, and is characterised by three elements:

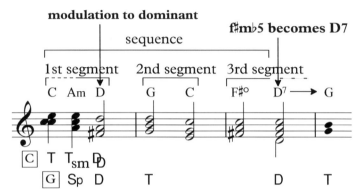

Ex. 93, ML: Short sequence, chords

1. The sequence starts on **Tsm**

2. The modulation to **D** tonality is already heard in the **1st segment**

3. The sequence is left in the **3rd segment** through the use of harmonic ambiguity. The diminished chord of the seventh degree of the **D** tonality is reinterpreted as **D7**, through the sounding of the root of the dominant in the bass (see also ex. 93, bar 3)

See also *Appendix B, sequences,* short sequence in major, page 101.

Theme III

Based on: alternative sequence ex. 89, page 73:

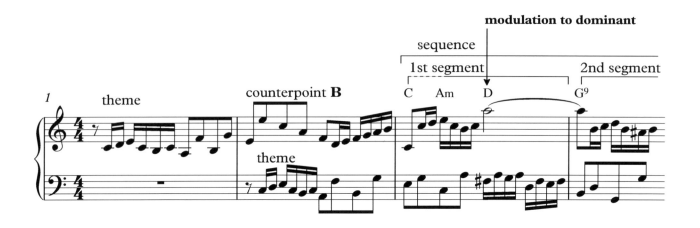

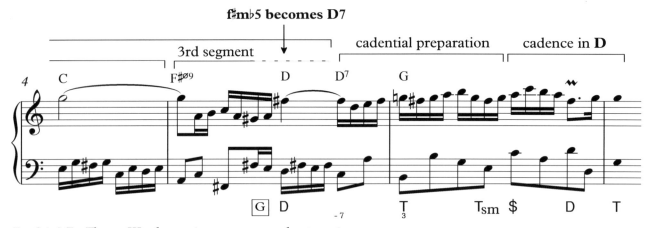

Ex. 94, ML: Theme III, alternative sequence – short version

As the sequence is quite short, a longer cadential preparation is required to lead from the sequence to the cadence in the **D** tonality.

Theme IV

Based on: sequence ex. 90, page 74:

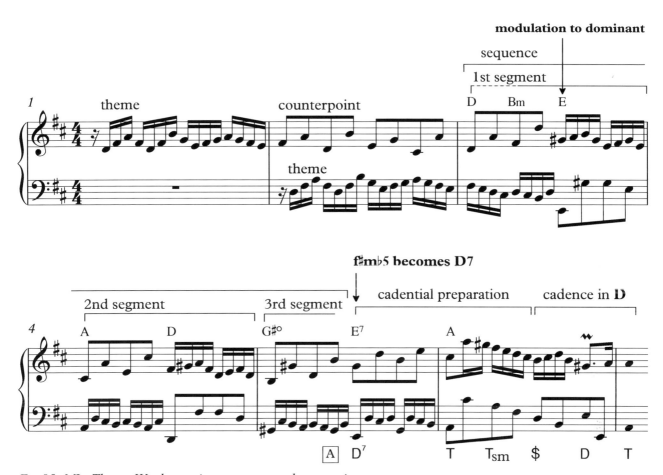

Ex. 95, ML: Theme IV, alternative sequence – short version

Bar 5 sounds like a long dominant to A major, leading to a culmination in bar 6, and which is resolved through a leap up to the top tone *a* in the soprano, followed by stepwise motion down to the cadence in A major.

Alternative solutions

Good alternatives to the first half of the major invention:

1. Answering at the fifth

2. Modulation to other tonalities than **D**

3. Other types of sequences

4. Canon

Answering at the fifth

As with the minor invention, answering at the fifth is almost as common as answering at the octave, and some themes even have an inbuilt modulation to the dominant, such as Bach's Invention no. 10 in G major, where the one-bar theme ends on the dominant. It is answered in the dominant, with an alteration of the theme, thus modulating back to the **T** in G major.

Alternative sequence

As with the minor invention, it's possible to use other types of sequences (see also *Episode without descending fifth sequence*, page 62).

Alternative to modulation to the dominant

When answering at the fifth, the dominant is visited. Thus, the first section of a major invention with answers at the fifth occasionally modulates to **Tp** instead of **D**. For example: Bach: Invention no. 5 in Eb major, bar 12 or Bach: Invention no. 12 in A major, bar 9 *(Appendix D, Bach invention, 1st section*, page 117).

Canon

Canon is a strict compositional technique, where a voice is imitated after a certain delay in another voice. The most common canon is at the octave (distance of an octave between the two voices), but any other interval can be used.

Canon (compositional technique)

When composing a canon, two elements must be decided: where the other voice should be, and how long the delay between voices is.

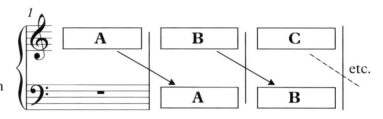

Ex. 96, ML: Canon (compositional technique)

In the case of a canon, such as in ex. 96, where the soprano is imitated an octave under in the bass after a bar, the first bar of the soprano (**A**) is placed in the second bar of the bass, an octave lower. A countermelody (**B**) is then composed. This is then placed in the third bar in the bass, and a new countermelody (**C**) is composed, and so on.

Completing the canon: *Theme IV*

Based on: Bach: Invention no. 8 in F major, bars 1-12, *Appendix D, Bach invention, 1st section*, page 116.

As mentioned under minor inventions, the canon principle often influences the form very significantly. In the next example (ex. 97), the soprano from bars 1-7 is imitated almost completely strictly in the bass, with the exception of a few small changes in the ending of bar 5 necessary to create a proper modulation to **D**. The episode in bars 3-5 is a pattern ascending by thirds, based on the counterpoint in bar 2 with a new bouncing figure in ♪ in the soprano.

In terms of the form, the descending fifth sequence is not heard until bar 8, where it leads from **D** to **Dp** in bar 11. Like the earlier descending fifth sequences in major, **Tsm** in the dominant tonality is used as a starting point, to be able to lead naturally to **Dp**.

Canon: Theme IV

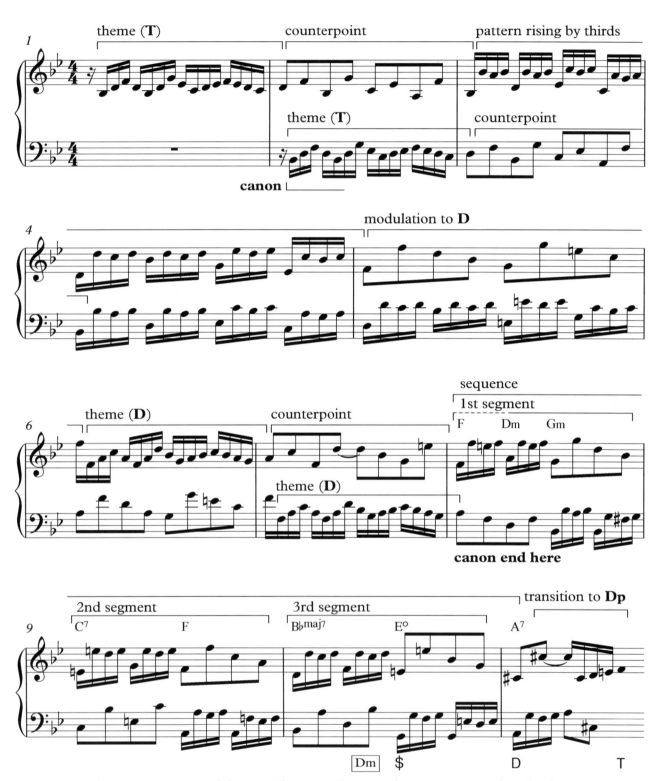

Ex. 97, ML: Theme IV, transposed down to Bb major: Canon and pattern in ascending thirds

Overview of examples

Appendix A, functional analysis, chords and chord symbols

In this book, *chord symbols* and/or *functional analysis* are used to illustrate cadences, harmonic progressions, etc.

Chord Symbols

Chord symbols are the simplest method of indicating chords. They show, in a natural and quick manner, the chord in question, the bass tone, and if there are any additions or alterations to the chord.

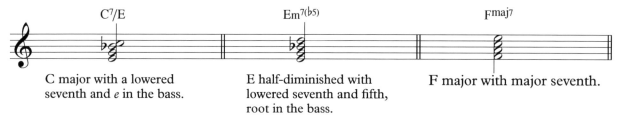

C major with a lowered seventh and *e* in the bass.

E half-diminished with lowered seventh and fifth, root in the bass.

F major with major seventh.

Ex. 98, ML: Chord symbols

However, chord changes fall short in terms of illustrating the chord relationships between individual chords in a harmonic progression.

Functional analysis

Functional analysis attempts to rationalise harmonic energy in tonal music through assigning individual chords a function in the tonality: resting **T** - tonic, tense **D** - dominant, and so on. Though this, the chords' affinity to one another is made clear.

Tonal music is based on the cadence, which through its three basic functions, **T** - tonic, **S** - subdominant and **D** - dominant (which leads back to **T**), form the basic skeleton of tonal music.

In cadences in tonal harmony, the affinity between **T** and **S** as well as between **D** and **T** is very distinct, due to the descending fifth from C major to F major and from G major to C major. This strong affinity arises from the common tone, the rising semitone, as well as the falling fifth in the bass.

The cadence can therefore be divided into two chord pairs: **T** to **S** and **D** to **T**, which both contain a strong fifth relation.

These chord pairs are separated by **S** to **D**, which, on the other hand, has a relatively weak affinity, as there are no common tones, only one falling semitone, and a lack of a falling fifth in the bass.

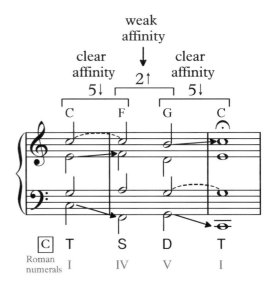

Ex. 99, ML: Cadences in tonal harmony

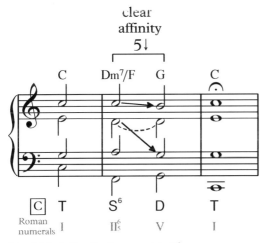

Ex. 100, ML: Cadence with S⁶

The weak affinity between **S** and **D** is a fundamental problem in cadences in tonal harmony, and many solutions have been proposed in countless ways through the history of tonal music, from the Baroque period to modern times.

The simplest solution has been to alter a single tone in the subdominant **S** (see ex. 100); the root in the alto has been altered from *f* to *d*, and thus, an added sixth is present in **S**. The chord can therefore be interpreted as a Dm⁷, with the third in the bass, and the affinity to G major is thus greatly intensified through the falling fifth relation from Dm⁷ to G.

Upon closer examination, a common tone has been established in the alto, and a falling fifth is present in the *d* in the alto to the *g* in the tenor. Also, the falling semitone from *c* to *b* in the soprano is intensified, as *c* is the seventh of Dm⁷ and therefore must be resolved to *b*.

Basic functions

As seen in the tonal cadance, there are three *basic functions* in a tonality.

Important: in a minor tonality, the dominant is a major chord.

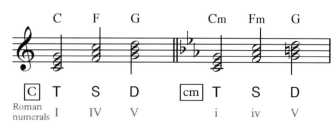

Ex. 101, ML: Basic functions

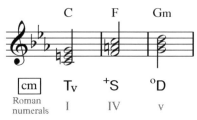

Ex. 102, ML: Variant and minor dominant etc.

A chord, whose quality has been changed, is known as a *variant*, For example, the tonic variant **Tv** in a C minor tonality is a C major chord.

In a minor tonality, the chord quality of **S** and **D** change relatively frequently, depending on the use of ascending or descending melodic minor passages. Therefore, they have their own indicators: *major subdominant* **⁺S** *og minor dominant* **ºD**.

First inversion chord (sixth chord)

In functional analysis, the bass tone will always be indicated below the function. If left blank, it is understood that the chord is in root position.

First inversion chords are chords with the third in the bass, which is indicated with the number '3' below the function.

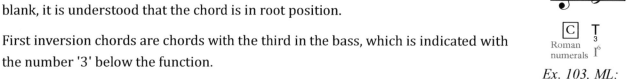

Ex. 103, ML: First inversion

Dominant seventh chord

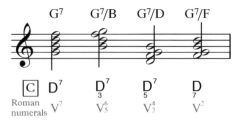

Ex. 104, ML: Dominant seventh chord

The seventh is a dissonance, which intensifies the dominant function of the chord (se also *The treatment of dissonance*, ex. 6, page 14). This is rather effective and gives all major chords with an added minor seventh a dominant function for a certain amount of time.

This chord can have any of the four tones in the bass.

Appendix A, functional analysis, chords and chord symbols

Incomplete dominant

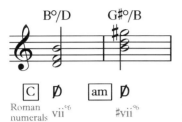

Ex. 105, ML: Incomplete dominant

The *incomplete dominant* is a dominant with a seventh, omitted root, and with the fifth in the bass.

Important: As the root is omitted, *f* is no longer a dissonance and therefore does not need to be prepared or resolved by a descending step.

Cadential chords

The *incomplete subdominant* is a **S** with added sixth and omitted fifth, and is the most common cadential chord in two-part movements.

It is seen both in the cadence and through the course of the invention, and is typically characterised through a falling third in the top voice, when the chord moves to **D**.

Ex. 106, ML: Incomplete subdominant

Ex. 107, ML: Cadential chords

The *Subdominant with added sixth* **S⁶** is occasionally used in two-part movements and is seen more frequently as the number of parts increase. It is mainly used in the cadence, but can also be encountered as a function in a harmonic progression. The fifth of the chord is a dissonant tone, and thus has to be prepared and resolved to the third of the dominant.

Dominant 4-3 and *dominant 6/4 suspensions* are exclusively cadential chords and cannot be used outside a cadence. In both chords, the fourth is the dissonant tone.

Note that in all three cadential chords, the root of the key is the tone that is prepared, suspended, and resolved by a downward step to the leading tone.

Parallel chords

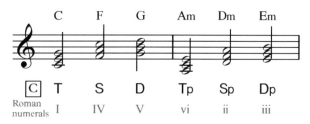

Ex. 108, ML: Parallel akkorder

The parallel tonality is the tonality with the opposite chord quality, but with the same key signature. For example, C major and A minor, C minor and Eb Major, etc. Parallel chords are indicated with a **p** after their function.

Note that **Dp** i in major is a minor chord, and not a major dominant, as is normal in minor. In other words, **Dp** in C major is an E minor chord and not an E major chord, as would be encountered in A minor.

Tonic submediant

The *tonic submediant* **Tsm**, is the most common use of parallel chords in tonal music from the Baroque to Romantic era.

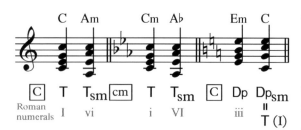

Ex. 109, ML: Tonic submediant

The tonic submediant is often approached through the repetition of tones and is realised by sounding the chord a third under the chord that has just been heard; a minor third in a major tonality and a major third in a minor tonality (ex. 109). The tonic submediant is most commonly applied to the tonic chord, but the same process can be applied to other chords in the Baroque style, for example **S – Ssm**, **Tp – Tpsm** and **Dp – Dpsm** etc.

Upon closer examination, (ex. 110), it is clear that only the fifth moves (and not the root or third). When the fifth rises a step, the quality of the chord is changed; a major chord becomes minor, and the minor chord becomes major.

The submediant is interpreted as a 'derivation', indicating that the two chords are not heard as a clear chord change, but rather as a change in nuance of the first chord due to the two common tones.

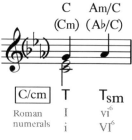

Ex. 110, ML: T - Tsm

Appendix A, functional analysis, chords and chord symbols

Tonic mediant

The tonic mediant is, as opposed to the tonic submediant, relatively rarely seen in tonal music.

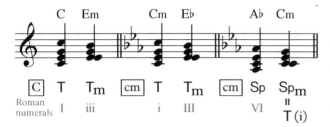

Ex. 111, ML: Tonic mediant

The tonic mediant uses the opposite motion as the submediant substitution. Thus, it lies a third **above** instead of below, and is commonly approached through a lead of a third in the bass and scalewise motion in the soprano.

Important: One of the defining differences between medieval modal harmony and tonal harmony is the use of the tonic submediant versus tonic mediant.

- **Medieval modal harmony**

  The tonic mediant, and occasionally submediant, is frequent, especially in root position.

- **Tonal harmony**

  Relatively infrequent use of the tonic mediant, but the tonic submediant is common.

Tonic substitution (deceptive cadence)

The *tonic substitution (deceptive cadence)* **Ts**, unlike **Tsm** and **Tm**, has a relatively strong harmonic effect: after a **D** a **T** is expected, but the chord a third under is sounded instead. In the same manner as the tonic submediant, **Ts** lies a minor third below **T** in a major tonality, and a major third below in

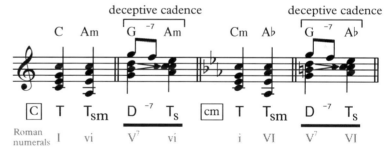

Ex. 112, ML: Tonic substitution (deceptive cadence)

minor. The third in the chord is normally doubled, partly due to the natural voice-leading, and partly to retain the character of the expected tonic: that the natural doubling of the root in **T** becomes a doubling of the third in **Ts** instead.

Secondary dominants

Dominants to all chords other than the tonic are called *secondary dominants*, and are indicated in brackets.

Ex. 113, ML: Secondary dominants

A special class of secondary dominant is the dominant to the dominant. It has its own function, indicated **DD**. It is also sometimes referred to as a double dominant.

Incomplete dominant ninth chord and altered dominants

In an *incomplete dominant ninth chord*, the root is omitted, as the clash between the root and the minor ninth is too harsh. The most common bass tone is the third, but the chord can have any of its tones in the bass.

Ex. 114, ML: Incomplete dominant ninth chord and altered dominant

Occasionally, the fifth is changed/*altered*. The diminished fifth leads down to the root, and the augmented fifth leads up to the major third of the next chord.

Neapolitan subdominant

The *neapolitan subdominant* **Sn** is a minor subdominant with a lowered sixth instead of a fifth, and is therefore identical in major and minor tonality. It is characterised by the presence of the lowered second degree of the tonality, that often melodically leads to the leading tone. For example, *db → b* in C major.

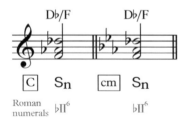

Ex. 115, ML: Neapolitan subdominant

Sn arose as a special aural effect in the Neapolitan operas in the first half of the 17th Century, and gradually became widespread and accepted as part of the standard harmonic vocabulary of the Baroque and Classical styles.

The neapolitan subdominant is commonly used towards the end of a piece.

Mediants

Mediants are chords whose roots are a third away from **T** or other functions. Mediants, like submediant or mediant substitution, can be used with other functions, such as **Dwsm** (=**Dm**), **Tphm** (=**TpM̄**) and so forth. The altered and double-altered mediants are very rare in the shorter works of Bach, including the inventions, but are occasionally seen the more harmonically complex works by Bach.

Traditionally, mediants are described in two ways:

1. By voice-leading (English and partly German tradition).
    Divided in 3 groups called diatonic-, chromatic- and double-chromatic-mediants[7]

2. By the size of the third between the fundamentals of the chords (German tradition). As in the English tradition, the mediants are divided into 3 groups called 1st order-, 2nd order- and 3rd order-mediants. The mediants in the 2nd and 3rd order (chromatic- and double-chromatic-mediants) are then further defined by the distance between the fundamentals of the chord (large third vs minor third).

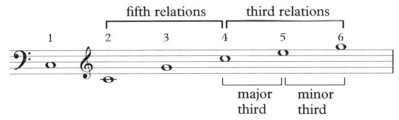

Ex. 116, ML: Chord relation in the harmonic series

The main chords **T**, **S** and **D** in the classical period are related by fifth (partial 2, 3 and 4 in the harmonic series). In the romantic period the major and minor third relations between chords (partial 4 to 5 and 5 to 6) gets more and more popular together with a higher use of chromatic- and common tones between the chords. In that way it makes sense to define the chromatic-mediants by the size (and direction) of the third distance between the fundamental of the chords rather than by voice-leading.

Naming and symbols

The English tradition lacks a division of the chromatic mediants respectively a major and a minor third from the original chord, and I have therefore added a distinction between this chords and named them A) *half-tone-* and B) *whole-tone-chromatic-mediants*. This distinction is important partly because the *half-tone-chromatic-mediant* is more frequent than the *whole-tone-chromatic-mediant*, especially in the

---

7   The defination "diatonic", "chromatic" and "double chromatic" mediants are used by Allan Forte in his *Tonal harmony in concept and practice* published by Holt, Rinehart & Winston of Canada Ltd.

earlier classical period, and partly because there is a significant difference in sound and musical expression.

In German tradition, they have this distinction, but do not have an independent symbol for mediants of the 2nd and 3rd order, but use other symbols from the functional analysis instead. Thus, in my opinion, they lose a significant interpretation of the special mediant relationships that gradually becomes an essential part of the character and expression in the romantic music.

In the following examples, I have 1) used an alternative symbol and naming used in the Danish music theory tradition and 2) used *triangels* and *squares* to indicate the relations in the *circle of fifths*.

1. **Diatonic-mediants** (shortly called mediants)
   As mentioned on page 91, the diatonic-mediants are the most common form of mediants, especially the tonic-submediant **Tsm** (see also ex. 111).

   The diatonic mediants has *opposing* chord quality and *2 common tones* with the **T** chord.

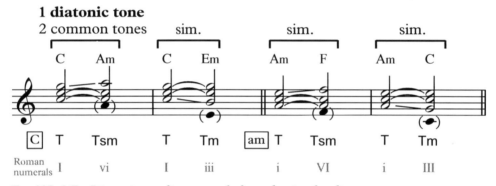

Ex. 117, ML: Diatonic-mediants, symbols and voice-leading

Notation: The diatonic mediants are notated as **Tsm** and **Tm**, respectively, and are closely connected in the circle of fifths.

Ex. 118, ML: Diatonic-mediants in the circle of fifths

2. **Chromatic-mediants**: Mediants with the *same* chord quality and *1 common tone* with the **T** chord, divided into:

Appendix A, functional analysis, chords and chord symbols

A) **Half-tone-chromatic-mediants** (shortly called half-tone-mediants).

- Always two chords a **major third** appart with the same chord quality.

  1 half tone/half step, 1 chromatic tone and 1 common tone

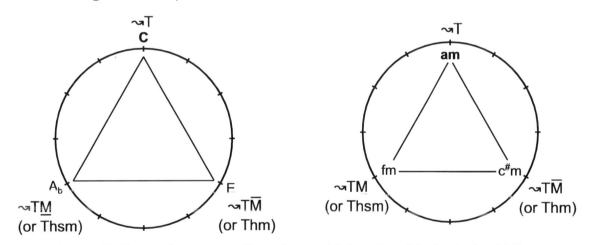

Ex. 119, ML: Half-tone-mediants, symbols and voice-leading

- **Best notation**[8]: large **M** for the major third (chromatic) mediant with a line respectively above or below to indicate whether it is a mediant or submediant

  - **Naming**: Major-third-(chromatic-)mediant/-submediant

- **Notation** based on voice-leading: Adding the letter *h* before m/sm

- notice how the half-tone-chromatic-mediants divides the circle of fifths circle into a triangle with a **major third** between the roots of the chords:

Ex. 120:, ML: Half-tone-chromatic-mediants (major-third-mediants) in the circle of fifths

---

8   The alternative notation: T$\overline{\text{M}}$ and T$\underline{\text{m}}$ etc., are proposed in this context as simple solutions, independent of language. The naming is derived directly from German (and Danish) music theory, with the addition of "third" to clarify the chord.

B) **Whole-tone-chromatic-mediants** (shortly called whole-tone-mediants).

- Always two chords a **minor third** appart with the same chord quality.
  1 whole tone/whole step, 1 chromatic tone and 1 common tone

1 whole tone
1 chromatic tone
1 common tone

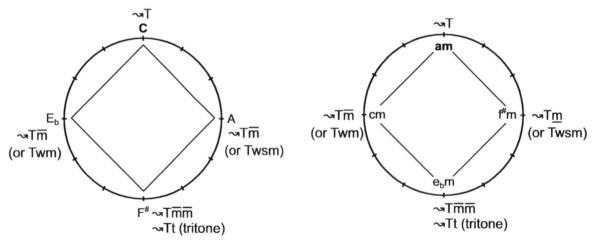

Ex. 121, ML: Whole-tone-mediants, symbols and voice-leading

- **Best notation**: Small **m** for the minor third (chromatic) mediant with a line respectively above or below to indicate whether it is a mediant or submediant

  - **Naming**: Minor-third-(chromatic-)mediant/-submediant

- **Notation** based on voice-leading: Adding the letter *w* before m/sm

notice how the whole-tone-chromatic-mediants divides the circle of fifths circle into a square with a **minor third** between the roots of the chords:

Ex. 122, ML: Whole-tone-chromatic-mediants (minor-third-mediants) in the circle of fifths

3. **Double-chromatic-mediants** (shortly called double-mediants)

Mediants with *opposing* chord quality and *no common tones* with the **T** chord

2 chromatic tones, 1 half-/ or whole tone and no common tones

These chords have a very strong harmonic effect, and is seldom used in classical music. Note that there are only two double-altered mediants in both major and minor.

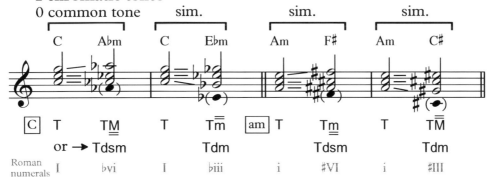

Ex. 123, ML: Double-chromatic-mediants, symbols and voice-leading

Best notation: Use *two lines* respectively above or below the letter **M/m**

• **Naming**: Major/minor-third-dobbelt-chromatic-(sub)mediant *or* Major/minor-third-(sub)mediant-in-major/minor

Notation based on voice-leading: Adding the letter *d* before m/sm

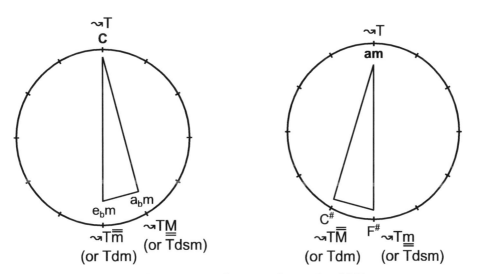

Ex. 124, ML: Double-chromatic-mediants in the circle of fifths

Appendix B, sequences

Overview of common sequences in episodes, which lead from the first entry of the theme in the **T** tonality to the cadence in **Tp** tonality (minor invention) and **D** tonality (major invention).

Minor invention – first section

Two typical methods in minor (see also page 43-56):

1. Descending fifth sequence with part redistribution

2. Descending fifth sequence with acceleration of harmonic rhythm

Descending fifth sequence with part redistribution

Descending fifth sequence with four to five segments, which lead from **T** to the cadence in **Tp**. Variation in 3rd segment through redistribution of one part, typically by moving the soprano to the bass (see als page 52-53).

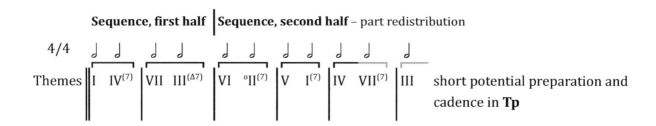

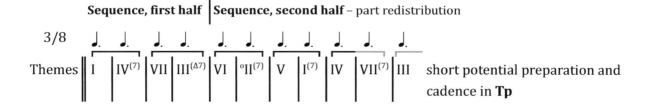

Example in A minor

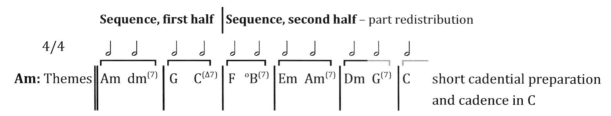

Appendix B, sequences

Descending fifth sequence with acceleration of harmonic rhythm

Descending fifthe sequence with four to five segments, leading from **T** to cadence in **Tp**. Variation in 3rd segment by accelerating the harmonic rhythm, but retaining the motivic material (see also page 54-56).

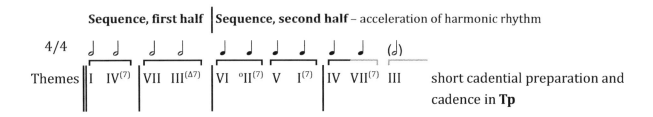

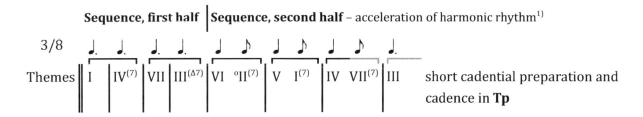

[1] With two chords per bar in 3/8, the chord rhythm | ♩ ♪| is typically used, but the retrograde rhythm | ♪♩ | is also possible.

Example in A minor

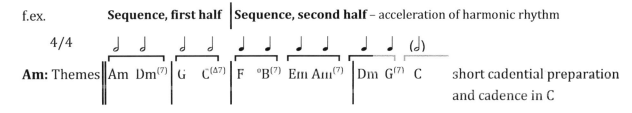

Major-invention – first section

Two typical methods in major (see also page 71-79):

- Descending fifth sequence, long version with variation

- Descending fifth sequence, short version

Important: In both versions, the sequence does not begins with the tonic, but with its derivation (chord on the VI degree).

- **4/4: Tsm** is normally derived from **T** through the course of one ♩, and the chord on the II degree is heard on the third beat of the bar. Occasionally, **T** is heard on the first beat, **Tsm** on the third beat, and the II degree chord is only heard on the second bar.

- **3/8: Tsm** is derived from **T** through the course of a bar, and the second degree chord is heard on the next bar.

Descending fifth sequence, long version with variation

Descending fifth sequence in four to five segments, starting with **Taf** (chord on the VI degree). As in minor invention with variation in the 3rd segment through either part redistribution or acceleration of harmonic rhythm (see also page 75-76).

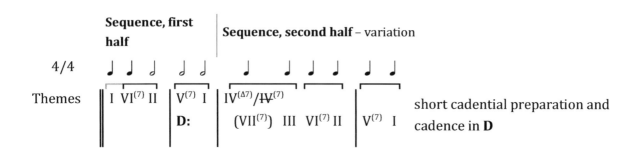

Example in C-dur

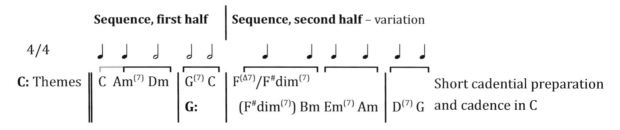

Descending fifths sequence, short version with harmonic ambiguity

Descending fifth sequence in five segments starting with **Tsm** (chord on the VI degree), where the diminished VII degree chord in the dominant tonality is supplied with a root, thus becoming **D⁷** (see also page 77-79)

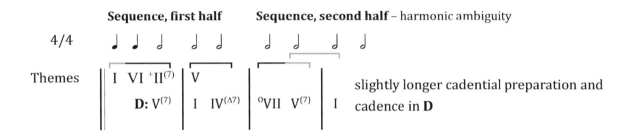

Example in C-major

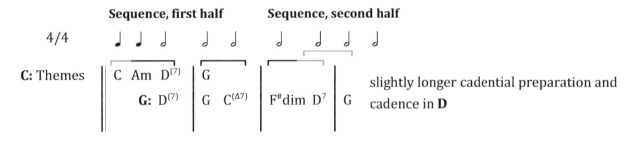

Appendix C, all examples

Inventions, first section worked on in *Volume I*

Theme I (E minor), sequence with part redistribution

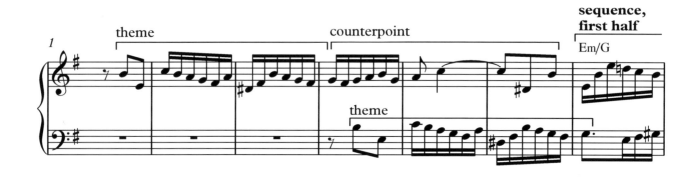

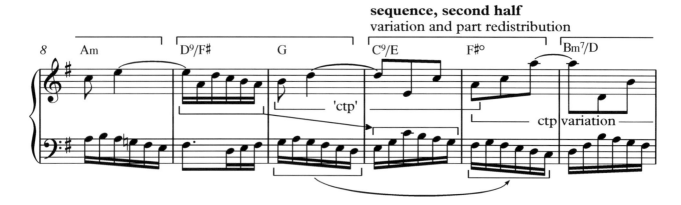

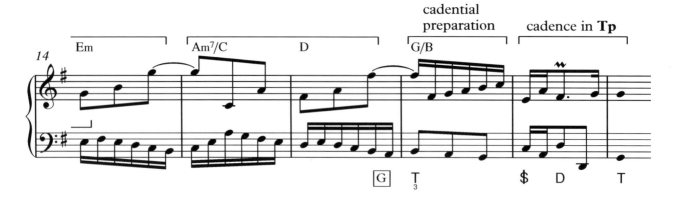

Theme I (E minor), sequence with acceleration of harmonic rhythm

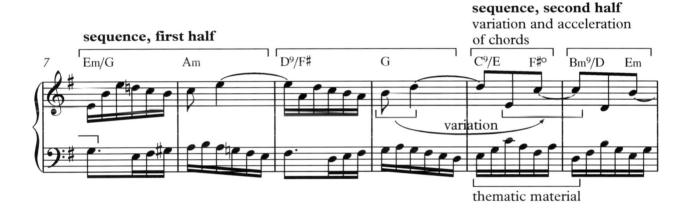

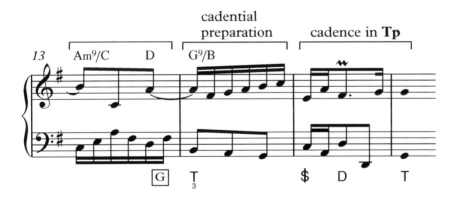

Theme II (D minor), sequence with part redistribution

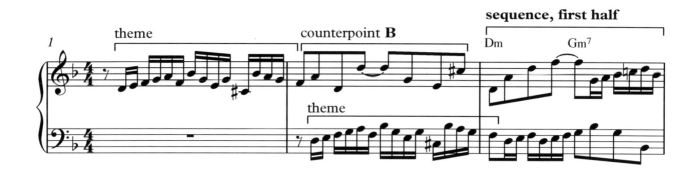

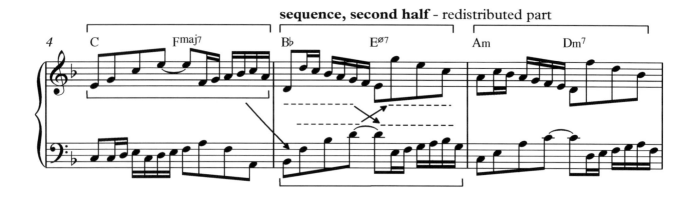

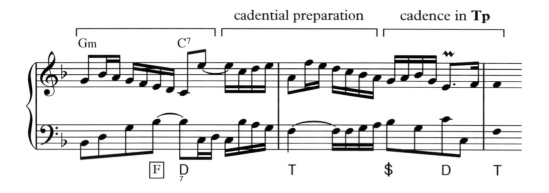

Theme II (D minor), sequence with acceleration of harmonic rhythm

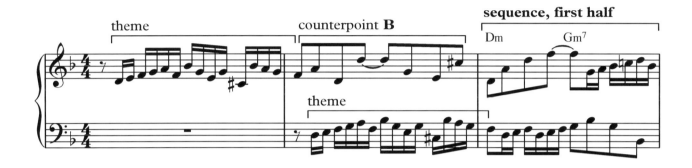

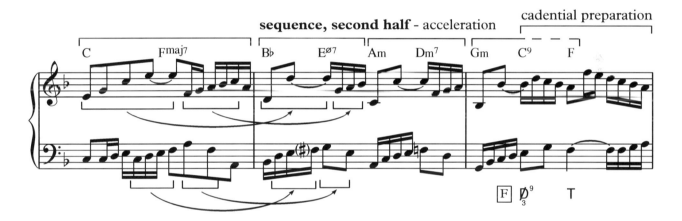

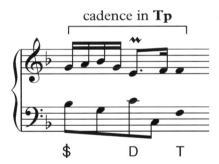

Theme II (D minor), sequence with broken chords and acceleration of harmonic rhythm

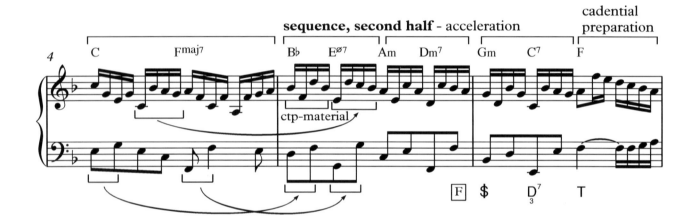

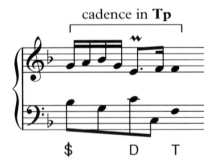

Theme I (E minor), answer at the fifth and sequence

Theme III (C major), long sequence, version I

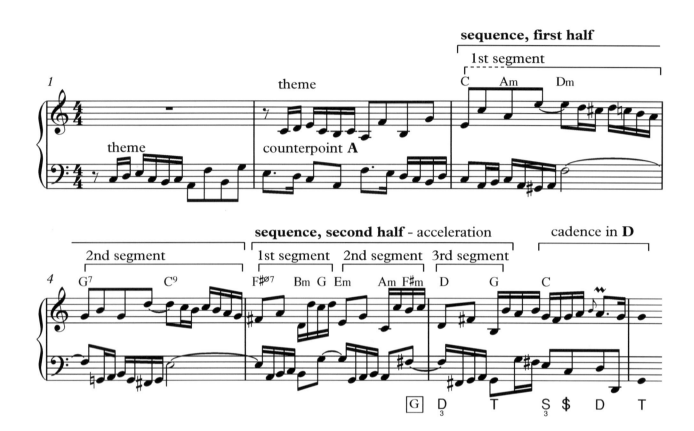

Theme III (C major), long sequence, version II

Theme III (C major), short sequence

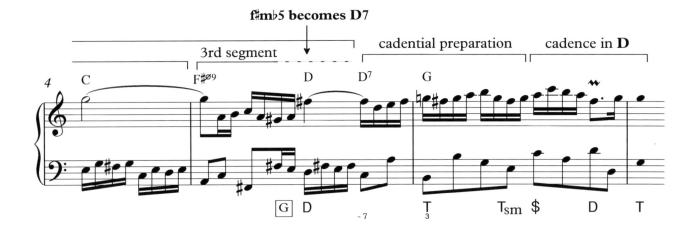

Theme IV (D major), short sequence

Theme IV (B♭ major), canon

Appendix C, all examples

Appendix D, Bach invention, 1st section

Bach inventions – 1st section up to entry in **Tp** (minor invention) or **D** (major invention).

Bach: Invention no. 4 in D minor, bars 1-18

Johann Sebastian Bach

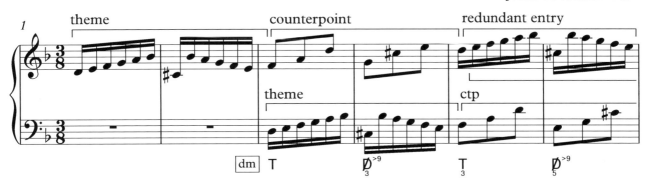

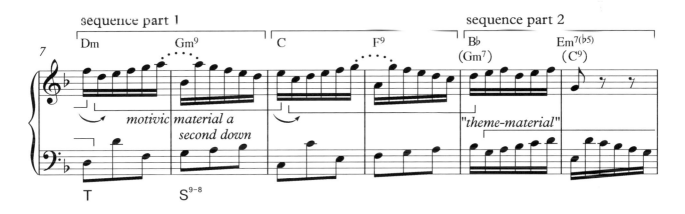

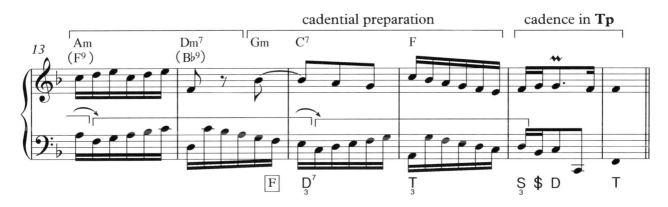

Bach: Invention no. 13 in A minor, bars 1-6½

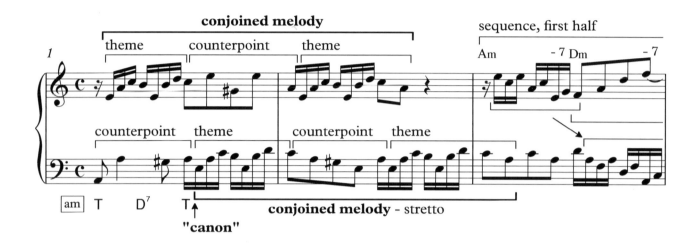

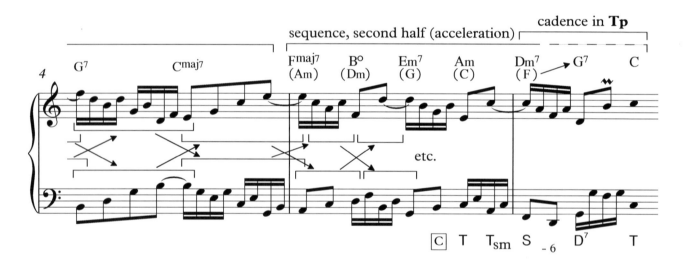

Bach: Invention no. 6 in E major, bars 1-20

Johann Sebastian Bach

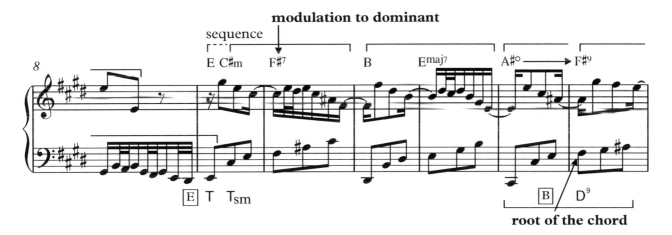

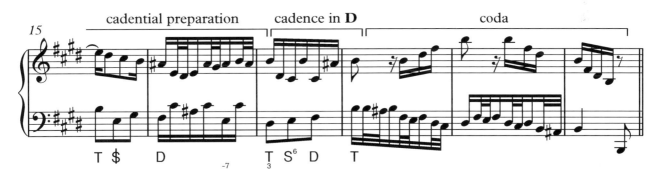

Bach: Invention no. 8 in F major, bars 1-12

Johann Sebastian Bach

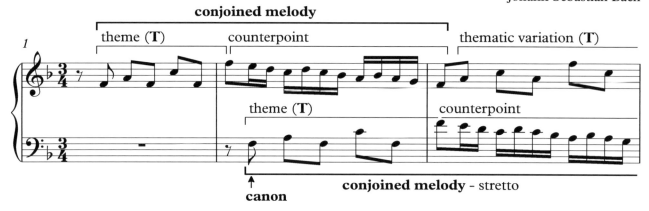

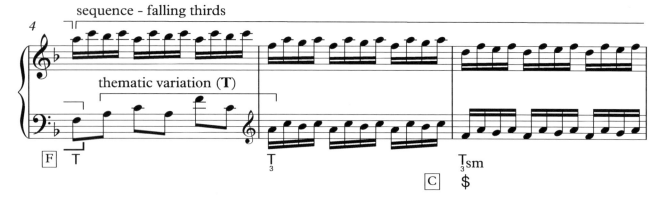

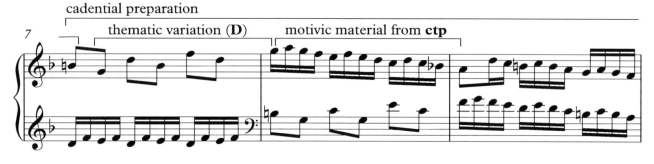

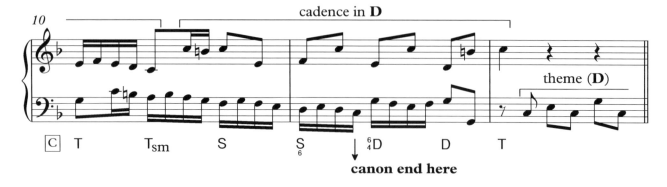

Bach: Invention no. 12 in A major, bars 1-9

Appendix E, themes

Themes used to illustrate examples in *Volume I* (two-part invention in the style of Bach, first section) and *Volume II* (complete two-part inventions in the style of Bach).

Themes from examples

Theme I *in E minor, used in Volumes I + II*

Theme II *in D minor, used in Volume I*

Theme III *in C major, used in Volume I*

Theme IV *in D major or Bb major, used in Volumes I + II*

Theme V *in C major, used in Volume II*

Theme VI *in G major, used in Volume II*

Medium-length themes for exercises

Themes in relatively fast tempo, for use in exercises in creating the first section of a two-part invention in the style of Bach (*Volume I*) as well as complete two-part inventions (*volume II*)

*Exercise theme 1: **ML**: Fast theme, best with answer at the octave*

*Exercise theme 2: **Bach** (in a reduced version): Fast theme, best with answer at the octave*

*Exercise theme 3: **Bach** (in a reduced version): Fast theme, best with answer at the octave*

*Exercise theme 4: **Bach**:Fast theme, best with answer at the octave*

*Exercise theme 5: **Bach**: Relatively fast theme, best with answer at the octave*

Exercise theme 6: **Bach**: *Relatively fast theme, best with answer at the octave*

Exercise theme 7: **Bach**: *Relatively fast theme, best with answer at the octave*

Exercise theme 8: **ML**: *Fast theme, suited to answer at the octave or fifth*

Exercise theme 9: **ML**: *Fast theme, suited to answer at the octave or fifth*

Exercise theme 10: **ML**: *Fast theme, suited to answer at the octave or fifth*

Exercise theme 11: **Bach** *(shortened): Fast theme, suited to answer at the octave or fifth*

Appendix E, themes

*Exercise theme 12: **Bach**: Relatively fast theme, suited to answer at the octave or fifth*

*Exercise theme 13: **Bach**: Relatively fast theme, suited to answer at the octave or fifth*

*Exercise theme 14: **Bach**: Fast theme, suited to answer at the octave or fifth*

*Exercise theme 15: **Bach**: Relatively fast theme, suited to answer at the octave or fifth*

Exercise theme 16: Bach: Fast theme, answer at the fifth

Short themes for exercises

Themes suited to 'conjoined melodies' and stretto, as described in *Volume II: further progress,* invention with short theme.

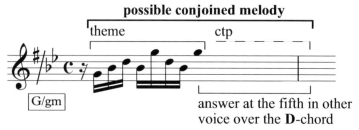

Exercise theme 17: **ML:** *Fast theme, suited to ´conjoined melody'*

Exercise theme 18: **ML:** *Fast theme, suited to ´conjoined melody'*

Exercise theme 19: **Bach:** *Relatively fast theme, suited to ´conjoined melody'*

Exercise theme 21: **Bach:** *Fast theme suited to ´conjoined melody'*

Exercise theme 20: **Bach:** *Fast theme suited to´conjoined melody'*

Exercise theme 22: **Bach:** *Fast theme suited to ´conjoined melody'*

Long themes for exercises

Long themes where the counterpoint is often heard together with the first entry of the theme.

Exercise theme 23: **Bach**: *Relatively slow theme suited to answer at the octave or fifth*

Exercise theme 24: **Bach**: *Relatively slow theme suited to answer at the octave or fifth*

Exercise theme 25: **Bach**: *Fast theme suited to answer at the octave or fifth*

Exercise theme 26: **Bach**: *Relatively fast theme suited to answer at the octave or fifth*

Exercise theme 27: **Bach**: *Fast theme suited to answer at the fifth*

Index

D

E

Printed in Poland
by Amazon Fulfillment
Poland Sp. z o.o., Wrocław

34612841R00076